PARENTING WITHOUT GUILT

PARENTING WITHOUT GUILT

AVOIDING 7 Things
Parents Do To Screw-up
Their Kids

Tom Couser

Outskirts Press, Inc.
Denver, Colorado

Outskirts Press, Inc.
http://www.outskirtspress.com

ISBN: 978-1-4327-4031-3

Outskirts Press and the "OP" logo are trademarks belonging to Outskirts Press, Inc.

PRINTED IN THE UNITED STATES OF AMERICA

Table of Contents

Words from the Author

During my early years as a church youth director and DCE it wasn't uncommon for people to ask, "So what are you going to do when you grow up?" Usually the question was posed with some tact but the intent was always obvious. Just how long do you intend on gaining much of your professional affirmation from working with teenagers? I guess it was difficult to identify with a grown man who still kept a squirt gun and whoopee cushion in his desk drawer.

It was a little easier for people to identify with me when I moved on being a high school counselor. Even then people often inquired as to how long I intended to work with kids. There reached a point when I guess I started to show my age, even if I didn't always act it. Then the questions became, "So what are you going to do when you retire?" Somewhere along the line my answer to that inquiry became, "I am going to write a book about my experience titled The Seven Things Parents do to Screw up their Kids."

When that day finally came some of my friends and former colleagues actually challenged me to put my money where my mouth is. "When's the book coming out?' they would ask. Almost two years later, here it is.

I need to thanks a number of people for helping me make this project a reality. At the top of the list has to be my editor, Mindy Walz. Mindy not only pointed out my spelling and punctuation mistakes but offered insight in content as well. She also offered advice and encouragement on printing and marketing.

Another good friend, Christine Morris, developed the cover art. I also need to give Christine credit for coming up with the title. Christine also read the manuscript and offered helpful feedback.

For eleven years I had the opportunity to be in ministry in one of the most caring communities imaginable. I owe thanks to my former colleagues at Lutheran High School of Dallas*. Your care and compassion continue impact my life. I still miss you guys.

Lorraine Gohr, Ben Sheck, Cassie Shermbeck, Angie Roberts and Katie Couser all read and provided feedback on the initial manuscript.

I truly appreciated the opportunity I had to work with the youth at Crown of Life Lutheran Church in Colleyville, Texas, Bethel Lutheran Church in Dallas, Texas and Saint Paul Lutheran Church in Plano, Texas. The comments and discussion were helpful.

I am blessed to be part of a very caring church community at Crown of Life Lutheran Church in Colleyville, Texas. In addition to the youth director, Ben Sheck, I have appreciated the support and encouragement of Pastors Dave Jung and Tim Perkins. I am also grateful to the Sunday morning adult Bible class that allowed me to try to out the discussion guide on them.

---

*   Now Dallas Lutheran School but it will always be LHS to me.

For almost forty years I have had the opportunity to work with thousands of kids in a variety of settings. Some I have gotten to know on a personal level, others have been just faces that have passed through my life. I am especially indebted to those who have shared personal information and allowed me into their lives. Some of you were victims of dysfunctional families. Others had devoted parents who fell into one or more of the traps I highlight in this book. Many of you have overcome your situations and gone on to be successful adults. Others continue to struggle but like all of us, you live under God's grace.

I have tried to maintain confidentiality in writing this book. None of the stories are based on actual events. Any similarities between the characters in this book and real people are strictly coincidence.

Barb and I have been blessed with a wonderful family. You get to meet Peter and Mark briefly in the forward. I've already promised Katie she can have the forward to the next book all to herself. Thanks as well to our daughter-in-law Amy. She and Peter continue to provide new examples of Christian parenting. Thanks for sharing Andrew, Caleb and Jonathan with us.

Last, I dedicate this book of my wife, Barbara. For almost forty years she has been a blessing in my life. The fact that our kids have turned out so well is a testimony to her. I often struggled with the issue of balance when it came to ministry and family. As I share in the book, I fell into some of the traps myself. Peter, Mark and Katie have inherited more than just their mom's good looks. Thanks for being there and allowing me to pursue my dream through this book.

You can e-mail me at www.thomascouser@yahoo.com

Foreword

"Train a child in the way he should go,
and when he is old he will not turn from it."

Proverbs 22:6 (NIV)

We must admit, it's a challenging task to write a foreword for a book on parenting when the author is your dad. It is a risky thing on our dad's part since he has no control over what we might say. What a nightmare it would be for him if the foreword for this book written by his own sons talked about how checked-out or clueless he was as a parent. Or perhaps we might share that he did not support us as we grew up and began to make some key decisions about college or career. What if he tried to live his dream vicariously through us?

Well, here is the truth. The filters are off and we will shoot with you straight from the hip. Do you want to know what our dad's biggest mistake was in raising us? Here it is… he allowed us to be Chicago Cub fans. How could he let us suffer year after year knowing full well that the last time the Cubs won the World Series was in '08… 1908 that is! Seriously, we have been incredibly blessed by God to have two loving, caring and supportive parents who have followed Christ individually as well as collectively. That does not mean that life in the Couser home always resembled something right out of an episode of "Leave it to Beaver" or "The Cosby Show," but we agree wholeheartedly what we have been blessed. Our mom and dad were not perfect, but they allowed the Lord to lead them through their parenting, and as a result we now live ministry lives that often find us both thinking, "that's how mom would have handled it" or "I'll bet that's what dad would do."

I (Peter) have seen this most vividly as Amy and I parent our three boys. Having family devotion time and encouraging our children, even when needing to speak the truth in love, are things I have learned from them. I recall a special moment when I had my dad come and speak to my Christian fraternity while I was at TCU. He shared with the guys the importance of book ending his day in prayer and God's Word. I have never forgotten those words and I know that practicing those bookends is the best gift I can give my family, especially to my kids. Attending a men's conference together a couple of years after graduating from college was a defining moment in our relationship as well. It was during that weekend when we realized once again the importance of hugs and the verbal reminder of "I love you." Since that conference, we have never been shy about saying, "Love you, dad" or "Love you, son" to each other. Exchanging an embrace after a golf outing or another night at the ballpark with my sons is the normal thing. All three of my boys can attest (well at least two of them can, as the other is just learning how to talk!) to the fact that their dad loves to hug his boys and make sure they hear "I love you," from their dad as he tucks them in at night.

I (Mark) have benefited greatly from the Christian example that my parents have set for me. It is their influence that has given me the ability to minister to urban youth for the last five years in Dallas. Many youth I work with are from broken homes and in need of the Christ-like example for them to emulate. I am so grateful for my parents' honesty, their integrity, and their forgiving and firm parenting style. There is no doubt in my mind that caring, teachable parents are one of the greatest gifts to any child. No parent is ever done learning on how to improve their parenting skills. I am glad my parents cared enough about me and my siblings to put Christ first in our home. I look forward to being a loving, teachable parent to my own kids someday.

We hope you are blessed richly by this book. Thank you, mom and dad, for passing on the faith to your children! Thank you for modeling for us how to follow Christ, regardless of earthly circumstances. And thank you, Lord for blessing us with parents that we now as adults can truthfully say are not just our parents, but also our friends.

We love you, mom and dad.

Peter and Mark Couser

Introduction

You have been given the biggest job assignment of your life. It's a life-long commitment and the stakes are high. The hours are long, and the demands seem endless. You, however, are determined to stay the course. You are a parent and you want to be the best parent you can be. After all, what parent stands over the crib of a newborn child and thinks, "What can I do to ruin this child's life?" Most of us set out to do the right thing when it comes to our children. During almost forty years of working with teenagers and their families, I have seen some examples of bad parenting; but I have seen countless instances of good parenting. I have also observed some reoccurring mistakes that even good parents make. For this book I have identified seven of the most common errors. My hope is that in recognizing these mistakes and their possible repercussions you might grow closer to becoming the parent God called you to be.

Being a parent is a daunting task. Being the parent of a teenager only increases the stakes. There are new challenges as our kids discover new emotions and feelings they have never had before. There can also be a lot of frustration and apprehension. I recall discussing my job as a youth director with one of the senior member at the first church I served in southeast Missouri. "I don't understand why you bother. The best thing to do is ship them to an island when they turn thirteen," he noted. "If they can pass a sanity test then they can come back when they turn twenty-one."

I must admit that there were times during those early years when I remarked that there was no way I would ever have kids myself. Working with them was one thing, but having one of my own was not something I looked forward to. In time God blessed Barb and me with three children of our own. People often remark how well out kids have turned out. To be honest I think it was probably more a blessing from God than the result of our expert parenting. Reflecting back, however, I probably enjoyed Peter, Mark and Katie's teen and college years more than any other time. I believe the source of that pleasure could be found in watching them discover their gifts and finding ways to use them to God's glory. That does not mean the road was easy, but it is such a great joy to watch your kids set goals for themselves and then strive to reach them.

This isn't about our kids, however. It's more about what I've experienced and observed as I have watched families, including my own, struggle to raise kids in a complex and changing world. Being a teenager has always been a treacherous journey, but the stakes are higher and the risk greater today. We can talk about the fact that alcohol was around when we were teens or the fact that we had classmates who were having promiscuous sex before they graduated from high school. The reality is that we live in a different world today. The pressures and choices today's teens face include things we hadn't even heard of during our teen years.

Much has been written about how the media affects on teens. Certainly popular music, television and the movies can have a negative impact if they are allowed to control us rather than serve us. The same could be said for the cyber-world of the internet.

This book is not about the negative impact of our culture. The world we live in is a reality. It is what it is and we cannot change that. We can, however, prepare ourselves and be ready to react to it in a positive way. We can take steps to make sure our kids are making good choices and having a positive impact on the culture, instead of the culture negatively affecting them. Over the years I have discovered that parents make most mistakes out of ignorance. I have yet to meet a parent who intends to be a bad influence on his or her children.

The following chapters identify seven common mistakes parents make and the implications that could result. At the close of each chapter, I offer an action plan for correcting those errors. My intention is not to inflict guilt. As you will read, I have made some of the mistakes myself. Even if you are making some of the mistakes right now, it is never too late to change the course. As parents, we need to take the lead in making the changes. Most importantly, we need to rely on the guidance of the Lord to lead us in training-up our children. Pray and trust in the Lord's mercy to provide a covering for your mistakes. You surely have made mistakes – because God the Father is the only perfect parent.

The opening chapter identifies two reasons why it is important for us to make those changes and make them now. Teenagers are facing the challenges of adolescence sooner and they are not mentally or emotionally equipped to deal with them. We need to provide a safe and structured environment for our teens to mature and grow. We also need to stay informed about their ever changing culture. It's also important to have a basic understanding of how typical teenagers think, act and feel. My prayer is that this book is helpful in the process. Consider what is offered here and pray. Ask God to help you discern what advice and information you can use in your family to glorify Him. God the Father, the only perfect parent, won't lead you the wrong way. He also knows your heart and the heart of your child completely. He is the only Father who truly knows best.

1

Parenting with Guilt

Danny sat quite uncomfortably in a chair in the assistant principal's office while down the hall in another office one of the female school counselors tried to console his classmate, Judy. What had happened had even the experienced school administrator scratching his head. Danny was a good kid, an above average student who played sports and had never been a discipline problem. In the minds of his teachers he was no more impulsive than his eighth grade classmates. As the male assistant principal looked across the desk at the frightened student he really wanted to ask, "What were you thinking?" Experience told him that Danny probably didn't have a plausible explanation for his actions.

Danny had waited by himself around the corner from the girl's locker room after his third hour physical education class. Judy was his target, although in his mind she was more the object of his affection. When Judy passed by with two of her friends, he grabbed her by the arm and in one motion embraced her and planted a kiss directly on her lips. His victim's screams attracted a teacher who quickly responded. Danny was escorted to the office while Judy and her friends were instructed to follow behind. Once in the office, Danny was told to wait for the assistant principal while the teacher guided Judy to the counselor's office to be comforted. The two friends were instructed to wait until someone could talk with them and get their account of what had taken place.

Judy and Danny had been casual acquaintances. They crossed paths a couple of time during the day in math, history and, of course, P.E. In one of those classes they sat next to each other and had struck up an informal conversation. One evening they found themselves on-line at the same time and had traded instant messages. But there was never any indication Judy was interested in any more than a friendship. How could such a casual relationship lead to such an outlandish act?

I have often visited with parents of early adolescents who ask, "What has happened to my kid?" Their open and loving son/daughter has suddenly become quiet and withdrawn, even surly at times. The boy who had always viewed girls as a "yucky" distraction to be avoided or teased suddenly becomes infatuated, or even obsessed with them. Middle school students can be a lot of fun to be around, but they can also be very frustrating. One of the most often asked questions of those who work with or who are raising teenagers is, "What were they thinking?" A simple, but truthful response might be, "Maybe they weren't."

The Teenage Brain

To understand why teens are they way they are we need to begin to understand how the teenage brain operates. The human brain is a complex organ. It is one of the features that make us unique among God's creatures. While it makes up only 1/45 of the total weight of the body, it holds the most potential. The human body contains billions of neurons that carry messages to and from the brain. The greatest concentration of neurons is in the brain itself. There is a vast difference between the brain or a newborn and that of a mature adult. As a child grows, neurons establish connections and paths. The brain or a child or adolescent is very much a work in progress as those links are developed.

An easy way to look at the brain is to compare it to a three-story house. The brain stem and the parts of the brain around it make up the first level. The brain stem connects the spinal cord to the brain itself: Information from the remote parts of the nervous system travel along the spinal cord to the brain stem. There it is received and processed, then passed on to the appropriate parts of the brain. The brain stem also monitors our vital organs, allowing them to respond quickly to emergency situations. The second level is the mid-brain. The short-term or working memory is located here, but so is the limbic system. Our senses report what is happening around us and we respond to it. Third story of the brain is the cerebrum, including the frontal lobe where complex thinking takes place. The long-term memory is also here. The long-term memory is not only the storehouse of an endless source of information and data, but also contains images of past events and experiences. Memories become helpful in dealing with current situations.

There is an additional part of the brain, however. It's called the **pre-frontal cortex.** It connects the second and third stories, providing a link between our emotions and feelings and our long-term memory. The executive functions of the brain are in the pre-frontal cortex. This region of the brain orchestrates our thoughts and actions in accordance with internal goals. The pre-frontal cortex also controls our impulses. Current emotions are processed based on past experience stored in our long-term memory.

This is where the teenage brain is different. According to Dr. Jay Giedd of the National Institute of Mental Health, the prefrontal cortex is one of the last regions of the brain to develop.[1] In reality, teenagers are ill-equipped to make adult decisions. While they become better at it as they mature, not even college students have reached their full potential when it comes to life decisions. Pre-teens have even less ability when it comes to decision making.

Educational psychologist and researcher Kathie F. Nunley notes:

> A region of the pre-frontal cortex plays the role of arbitrator in making these critical decisions. It quickly sizes up the situation and makes a determination which they drives our behavior. It is the pre-frontal cortex then that tell us when to act on our anger, or curtail it, to eat the second piece of dessert or go without, to seek immediate gratification or hold off for the long-term.[2]

Recent research by Professor Janice Juraska and a team of graduate assistants at the University of Illinois shed more light on the adolescent brain. Juraska's study concludes that the number of neurons in the pre-frontal cortex of the brain actually decrease during adolescence. "The pruning away of unneeded or disruptive neural circuits appears to be as important as the development of new neural connections," Dr. Juraska states.[3]

In the case from the beginning of the chapter, our friend Danny had some amorous feelings toward Judy. As a young teen, this was probably a new experience for him. He lacked the ability to make a healthy choice about what to do with the strong emotions he had. His actions serve as an example of seeking immediate gratification with little or no thought to the consequences.

While it's difficult to prevent every spontaneous behavior, we can take steps to help early adolescents like Danny save themselves from embarrassment. The first step is to be aware of the early stages of puberty and to acknowledge them. This means discuss the feelings that accompany the maturation process. Making Danny aware of the strong sexual impulses he might experience might have helped him make a decision in favor of a more socially acceptable response. While it's important to make sure that young adolescents are in a supervised environment, it's not possible to have a teacher or administrator in every school hallway. That's why parents need to assume the primary responsibility for helping their teens prepare for such situations.

Early Puberty

Young Danny also had to deal with sexual thoughts and feelings at an earlier age than previous generations. Puberty is a physical right of passage. It is the point at which an individual passes physically into sexual maturity. Historically, puberty has been linked to early adolescence. Generally it takes place in the early teen years. The average age for girls in twelve and the average age for boys is fourteen. But even the casual observer can note that things have changed. For parents, it can be a bit scary when a second grade daughter gives the first sign of a budding breast, or we find pubic hairs in our fourth grade son's underwear.

Those in the medical field have also taken notice. In 2003, The Endocrine Society noted the possible advancement in the timing of puberty over the previous decade.[4] Precocious Puberty has always been an accepted medical condition. Precocious Puberty is the early onset of puberty, usually attributed to a child being overly obese or to some other medical condition. What is happened to this current generation is not isolated to a small group of overweight children, however. Pediatricians are very aware of what is happening to today's children. The Tanner Scale is the established way of tracking sexual development. Stage Two is the point at which females begin to develop breasts. According to the 2001 issue of *Pediatric Journal*, "twelve percent to fourteen percent of females have Tanner Two breast development or greater while at age eight." It further notes that the median age of the attainment of breasts in females has fallen to 9.5 – 9.7 years from a previous 10.5-11.3."[5] That means the typical female is experiencing puberty a full year earlier. Similar studies of males indicate a comparable trend. If there is some comfort it can be found in the fact that menarche, the point at which a girl has her first period, has remained unchanged. It still takes place around age twelve. The thoughts and feelings of being older are present, however. If a young girl appears older than she is, it adds additional pressure. Others, especially older teenage boys, may think that she is more advanced in age than she looks. She may be more likely to end up in circumstances which are too difficult for her to handle well.

Puberty begins when a portion of the brain called the hypothalamus sends a message to the pituitary gland to release hormones. While we can identify the process, the exact reason for it beginning early remains elusive. Even the experts are still not able to identify a consistent cause for the early onset of puberty. The most common theory is that better nutrition has contributed to this trend. More recent research by R. Samuel McLaughlin at the University of Ottawa identifies environmental contaminants as the source. Some chemicals can mimic estrogen, the female hormone and accelerate the arrival of puberty.[6] The bottom line is that today's kids are facing difficult decisions regarding their sexuality at an earlier time and they are ill-equipped to handle them. The development of their bodies is outpacing the development of their brains.

Developing an Action Plan

NUTRITION

A proper diet is a key component in the physical development of children. We can begin by making sure our children are getting a balanced diet with daily foods from each of the major food groups. We need to limit the amount of fats they consume. Most fats come from what we call junk foods that contain empty calories. Doctors have identified a link between childhood obesity and precocious puberty.

EXERCISE

Insuring that our children are involved in some kind of physical activity is also vital. Children that have a sedentary lifestyle, watching television and playing video games, tend to become overweight. Limit the time in front of the TV and computer and get them involved in some kind of physical activity. One of our sons played basketball and the other soccer. Both also played baseball. Our daughter was involved in gymnastic at an early age. We found all these activities an excellent way for them to get exercise and have their own identity.

LIMIT EXPOSURE TO MEDIA

Media sources such as television, the movies and music can be a real blessing, but we need to control the amount of influence they have on our families, especially young children. Much has been written about the effects of violence on children, but the same could be said for programming containing explicit sexual content and objectionable language. We especially need to be aware of the impact television can have on children dealing with puberty issues. Do we want our fifth and sixth graders exposed to the sexual stereotypes portrayed on television?

AWARENESS AND OPENNESS

As responsible parents we need to be constantly aware of what is going on in the lives of our kids. Sudden changes in mood or behavior are reasons to ask questions. This becomes even more important as our children approach puberty. When the time is right a frank discussion about what we see and hear from them is important. Open conversation at an early age lets kids know that we are open to discussing sensitive topics later on.

Notes

1. Dr. Jay Giedd, Pediatrics 107 (June 2001); 1493
2. Kathie Nunley, "How the Adolescent Brain Challenges the Adult Brain, www. help4teachers.com/prefrontalcortex. htm

PARENTING WITH GUILT

3. www.eurekalert.org/pub_release/2007-03
4. Endocrine Review 24, Copyright 2003
5. Pediatrics 107, June 2001, pp. 1493
6. McLaughlin Centre, Institute of Population Health, University of Ottawa, info@emcom.ca

2

Mistake #1: Confusing Discipline with Punishment

Eli was a handsome, athletic high school student. His gregarious personality, outgoing nature and good looks made him popular with his peers and a favorite among the faculty at school. Eli lived with his single parent mom, who was a successful commercial real estate agent. They lived in a lavish home in a gated community. Eli always had spending money in his pocket. Eli and his mom had always had a good relationship. She was well educated and attractive, but because of her lifestyle Eli was left to fend for himself much of the time. Eli had never been a discipline problem, so he did not have many restraints.

Eli was only an average student. In the fall of his sophomore year he was failing two classes, which caused him to be ineligible for football. His mom responded by hiring a personal tutor and grounding him on weekends. Eli managed to pull his grades up and passed the semester, but ran into a similar issue in the spring. He became ineligible again, this time for baseball. Once again he was grounded. When he began to use his cell phone to text message his friends (something that was forbidden as part of the punishment) his mother confiscated his phone. This time Eli couldn't turn things around and he ended up failing biology. As a result he had to attend summer school. His summer schedule caused him to miss the daily morning sessions in the weight room, an expectation for all athletes.

When school started in the fall, Eli went out for football. His playing time was limited, though, because of his track record of having academic issues. When he met with the coach to discuss his status, the coach reminded him that he had started practices out of shape. The coach also mentioned his history of being ineligible. "I need players I can count on," the coach stated. Eli quit the team. With more time on his hands, Eli started hanging out with the friends he had met in summer school. One of them lived in a house close to campus where the kids could hang out after school. Eli told his mom he was going to his friend's house to study, but actually drugs and alcohol were readily available there. When Eli began to have academic issues again, his mom responded by grounding him again. This time Eli rebelled and he became angry and sullen. He locked himself in his room on weekends, not even coming out for meals. He spent his time playing video games and sleeping. Eli managed to pass his classes, so his mom lifted the restraints just before Christmas. Eli quickly returned to his friends and to the house close to school. It was shortly after the New Year when the local police showed up at the home where Eli and his friends hung out. Eli was arrested. As a result the school assigned him to an alternative program. As one requirement of the program, a school counselor met with Eli and his mom to help them develop a plan for turning things around.

Eli's grades and behavior did improve, so Eli was allowed to return to main campus for the fourth quarter. Things had changed, however, and his former friends were reluctant to spend time with him. As a result, Eli sought out his friends who were part of the drug culture. When the police picked him up for a curfew violation he found himself in trouble again. This time when his mom grounded him, Eli ran away from home. He returned to the drug culture and found refuge in an apartment occupied by college students who shared his addiction. His new companions were willing to let him stay there as long as he sold the drugs they gave him. Eli used his old contacts to become a major supplier at his former school.

One of the responsibilities of parenting is to discipline children, but many parents confuse discipline with punishment. One reason we do this is that punishment is easier. When our children do something wrong we respond with punishment. As a result the behavior discontinues. On the surface the problem has been solved. In actuality punishment can be self serving. The behavior which we find offensive or that projects the wrong image of us as parents is eliminated. What happens when the restraints of punishment are not there anymore? Our teens are not always going to be under our supervision.

Discipline

Discipline is defined as training, especially when it comes to mind and character. Discipline takes time and effort. Discipline, unlike punishment, has long-term effects.

The behaviors we observe are a result of the needs and values that an individual possesses. If we focus solely on changing the behavior, we are only dealing with the issue temporarily. Punishment might stop the negative behavior, but any change will not last. Once the threat of parental punishment is removed, children may feel they have no restraints. This explains why teens that were well behaved and successful in high school sometimes are suddenly out of control once they get to college. As a teenager, Eli lived in a world without boundaries. Boundaries tell a person where they can and cannot go. If you step over the boundaries, there are consequences.

Since Eli's behavior had never been a problem, his mother felt no need to place restrictions on it. She did not anticipate the changes in environment and the academic challenges that accompany being in a high school setting. As long as Eli was involved in athletics, there was structure in his life. When he quit the football team the structure disappeared and he didn't have the self discipline to handle the new freedom. When he started to struggle again his mom punished him. The behavior stopped but the problem did not go away.

Establishing a set study time at home and using a planner to track assignments are specific things Eli's mom could have done when his grades began to slip. She could have established boundaries with regard to his activities after school. His academic struggles could have opened the door to a discussion between mom and son concerning his long-range goals. They could have discussed where he wanted to go in life and how he was going to get there.

Boundaries tell a person where they can and cannot go. If you step over the boundaries there are consequences. Parents have the false impression that their teens don't like rules, when in fact they appreciate them. Boundaries and rules allow teens the freedom to function safely within their world. In Eli's case, boundaries would have helped him safely function in his world without the structure of football. By monitoring his behavior and providing adequate, not extreme, restrictions his mom could have helped him avoid the drug culture that exists in the teen world.

Dr. Walt Larimore, author of *Discipline and Your Teen*, notes:

> Lifting up our teens with affirmation, blameless love, and connectedness is critical for their [teenagers] health. But like a table, a fourth leg is needed to keep things on in equilibrium – the leg of parental guidance and enforced boundaries. If teens are to stay safe and healthy, your love must be balanced by and actively demonstrated through appropriate, loving discipline.[1]

Mark Gregston is director of Heartlight Ministries in East Texas. Mark heads a Christian residential counseling program for struggling teens. He notes, "Rules without relationship cause rebellion."[3]

Mark Gregston explains, "Your goal should be to establish a solid relationship, encouraging ongoing discussion, and as a result, other things that he struggles with will be revealed."[3]

In Eli's case, one of the boundaries should have been how he spent his time after school. If his mom had been monitoring his grades she would have caught on to the fact that he was not "studying with friends" after school. A boundary would have been requiring him to come home after school. A phone call once he arrived would have not only told his mom he was safe at home, but provided the opportunity to talk about the day and clarify his strategy for getting his homework done. With today's technology, caller I.D. would have also provided his mom with proof he was where he should be.

What happens when boundaries are crossed? I personally do not like the term punishment. Rather, I prefer the word consequences. Let's say Eli failed to call his mom one afternoon. The consequence might be the loss of a privilege, such as getting to play video games once his homework was done that evening.

Some consequences are natural. If teenagers experiment with drugs, they risk addiction. Other consequences are effectual, imposed by the community or group. In Eli's case the imposed consequences were that his former school friends isolated him and his mother grounded him and took away his cell phone. Even if these restraints had been successful and Eli had passed his classes, stayed drug free, and graduated from high school, there is the possibility Eli would have fallen into his old patterns during his college years or as a professional. What Eli needed most was boundaries established by a parent who was actively involved in his life.

If there was ever a time when kids needed boundaries it is now. The stakes are so much higher. Our teens live in a culture where everything is relative. As a result, traditional ethics and values have been called into question and, as we have already learned, teens are ill-equipped to make decisions in their changing world.

Guidelines to Setting Effective Boundaries

UNDERSTAND THEIR CULTURE

At some time most parents have used the line, "When I was your age…" in dealing with their teens. It doesn't apply today. None of us faced the challenges and ethical dilemmas that today's teenagers do. In today's world everything is relative. This is a trend that began in the seventies with the term "situational ethics." Right and wrong is determined by the situation. A generation later our culture has taken situational ethics to another level.

Situational ethics states that there is a right and wrong, it is merely determined by the desired outcome of the situation. Situational ethics is different from moral relativism in that moral relativism implies that there is no right or wrong.[2] In the teen world everything is relative. Relativists claim that humans can understand and evaluate beliefs and behaviors only in terms of their historical or cultural context.

The historical and cultural context of today's teens allows for a certain degree of cheating. The perceived unrealistic expectations of teachers, coaches and parents put students in the position where they believe they have to cheat. Since most of their peers cheat, and academic competition among those peers is so intense, it is in their best interest to cheat as well. To not cheat would put them at a disadvantage. But, are they being truthful to themselves?

The Roman Catholic Church, especially under John Paul II and Benedict XVI, has identified relativism as one of the most significant moral problems of today.[4] In the context of relativism it is easy to understand why in the minds of many teens, cheating is not wrong. To relate to our teens we need to understand their cultural context. In the "old fashioned" value system cheating was wrong even if some people, including ourselves, did it. In the current value system cheating is an acceptable behavior, required just to keep up.

PARENTING WITHOUT GUILT

Communicate the Why to the Boundaries

It's not enough just to establish rules and boundaries. Today's teens must also understand why those boundaries are important to them and to us. In communicating the reasons behind the boundaries, we are giving them insight into our values and showing that we respect and want to understand their values, as well.

Take one of the most common boundaries, curfew. The, "As long as you live under my roof you will be in by midnight," rationale for a curfew doesn't carry weight with a modern teen. In fact it will probably result in rebellion. Most communities have a curfew for teens under a particular age. That makes for a good starting point when explaining our motives. For an underage teen to be out after curfew is against the law. Obeying the law is part of being a good citizen. We might also point out that the criminal element in our society is most active after midnight. More DWI arrests and accidents take place after midnight. If we are going to state our case, we need to allow them to talk about what they might want to do after curfew. In listening to them we have shown that we are interested in them and their culture. We are also communicating that we care.

Choose Your Battles

Sometimes it seems as if living with a teenager means nothing more than existing with ongoing conflict. Just by human nature, two people living under the same roof are going to get on each other's nerves once in a while. When the rapid changes and the conflicting feelings of adolescence are added, it only increases the tension. Couples who have lived together for years still complain about each other's annoying habits -- like underwear on the floor or make-up left sitting on the bathroom vanity.

CONFUSING DISCIPLINE WITH PUNISHMENT

We need to remember this in dealing with our teens. Is having a clean closet really all that important, as opposed to having a perfect driving record behind the wheel of the family car? The bottom line is to focus on the issues that might be dangerous for your teen or others or might jeopardize their futures.

Clothing styles almost always will be an issue between parents and teens. Keep in mind that clothing styles are really a matter of personal taste and, unless they border on immodesty, should not be an issue. Every generation has their share of fashion trends that cause older folks to shake their heads in disbelief. Acknowledge that and let kids be kids. For many of them their hair styles and clothing are just a form of expression. For the most part, fashion trends are not worth the battle.

CONTROL YOUR TEMPER

One fit of temper can devastate a relationship that has taken years to build. This is a lesson I can confirm based on personal experience. As a school counselor I have spent years building a relationship with a student, only to have that destroyed by one incident where I lost my temper. It's a reality, kids will do things that make you mad – but then so do adults sometimes. Learn to live with it.

My experience also reminds me that most often my anger is a reaction to my own feelings. If I take a risk and trust a student and he or she lets me down, I get angry. As I examine my anger I have to admit that it's rooted in the fact that I feel I have been let down or, worse yet, made to look foolish. In the case of parents, often the anger is rooted in the fact that the behavior of our teens makes us look bad.

I have two words of advice when it comes to anger. First, focus on the behavior, not the person. Everyone makes mistakes. When that happens, focus on the mistake and what went wrong. Help the offender understand why it happened and what can be done to insure that it doesn't happen again. One of my favorite questions to students is, "So, what can we do so this doesn't happen again?" Second, think before you react. Even taking thirty seconds before reacting verbally provides time to process what is taking place. Most often I get myself in trouble when my reaction is spontaneous.

Learn to Forgive

As a Christian, I have learned that I live under grace. God forgives me for my sins and shortcomings. I need to apply the same principle to my relationship with others. This is especially the case for parents. Our children are gifts from God. From a biblical perspective, I have always liked the parable of the prodigal son (more appropriately, the forgiving father). The son asks for and receives half of his father's inheritance, which he then promptly blows on "wine, women and song." In desperation he finally decides to return home, not to ask for forgiveness, but to ask for a position as a servant. What he finds is a father who loves him, takes him back and forgives him unconditionally.

For me as a parent and, professionally, as a counselor, I need to be forgiving. I can be disappointed, frustrated, and angry, but I must always be forgiving. I need to express feelings of anger, but they must be in relationship to the behavior. Taking a, "This is what you did and this is the way it makes me feel," approach can work well. If expressed in that way, it provides the offender the opportunity to say, "Yeah, I screwed up. Please forgive me." In that case the relationship might be strengthened instead of harmed.

CONFUSING DISCIPLINE WITH PUNISHMENT

The bottom line is that our kids will always be our kids. We need to learn to love our child for who they are, not who we would like them to be. Like in other relationships, there are times and circumstances where the offender can't or won't take ownership of his or her behavior. In such cases we need to let the offense go and wait patiently, hoping the offender will eventually see the error of his or her ways.

Developing an Action Plan

SET REALISTIC BOUNDARIES

Because of the world we live in and the decisions that our teenagers face, parents need to establish realistic boundaries. Boundaries are the way we insure our teen's safety and hopefully long-term success. Establishing boundaries is not enough, however. Knowing what we do about the way the teenage brain operates, we need to be ready to help our teens make wise decisions despite the temptations and emotions they feel.

GET PERSONALLY INVOLVED IN YOUR TEEN'S LIFE

In Eli's case, instead of helping him work through the problem, his mom hired a personal tutor who could do it. That is what his mom was accustomed to doing in her professional life, so she applied the same thing to her personal life. There are a lot of great resources out there that support families with teens. In additional to personal tutors we could add college consultants, parent coaches, counselors, and clergy and school personnel. Ultimately, however, the responsibility to establish the boundaries and determine the consequences falls to the parent. When issues arise we need to sit down with our teens and discuss them. Conflicts are really growth points. You need to be growing in your knowledge of your teenager and they need to be growing in their ability to make good choices.

COMMUNICATE

Boundaries must not be seen as obstacles, but rather, opportunities. They should not block communication, but open the door to it instead. Parents need to be able to communicate their values and expectations, passing them on to the next generation. Communicate your needs, but listen to the needs of your teenager, as well.

REMEMBER WHO YOU ARE TALKING TO

Our teenagers are still our kids. It was probably easier to love them when they were infants and toddlers or even when they were in Kindergarten and elementary school. We had control and could manage their lives. The teen years mean more freedom and responsibility. As they change and develop their own lifestyles and even value systems it's easy to forget that they are our flesh and blood. When they do things that offend and even hurt us, we need to put aside our feelings and focus on the behavior and not the person. Words said in anger can cause irreversible harm.

NOTES

1. Discipline and Your Teens, Dr. Walt Larimore, www.crosswalk.com
2. www.gotquestions.org/situational-ethics
3. www.wikipedia.org
4. www.nationalcatholicreporter.org

3

Mistake #2: A Failure to Communicate

Samantha's parents referred to her as "God's Little Surprise." Samantha's sister was twelve years older, her brother older still. Her mother was a college English professor, her dad a successful attorney. They had a very comfortable lifestyle and Samantha never lacked for anything. They were active in their church. Her dad was on the church board. Her mom organized and led mission trips to a village in Mexico twice a year. Samantha was active in the church youth group and sang in the youth choir.

Samantha was a good student who was active in the school drama club. She helped to build sets and worked on the stage crew for every production. Samantha was pretty in a plain and simple kind of way. She was shy around people she did not know. Samantha did struggle with her weight and often tried to diet, but never with much success.

Samantha had a small group of friends, all other drama folks. The group was mostly female, but a couple of guys also enjoyed hanging out with them. Dating was never an issue. None of the girls had ever had a serious relationship with a boy and they jokingly referred to themselves as "The Virgins."

In the fall of her junior year a junior boy started flirting with Samantha. He was also in the drama club, but unlike her friends who worked behind the scenes, T. J. was an actor. He usually had major roles in the productions. Due to his outstanding vocal ability, he did especially well in musicals. Samantha's friends did not like T. J. because he had a reputation as a Romeo who moved from girl to girl. Samantha, however, was enamored with T. J. She had never had a boy show any interest in her before and she liked the attention. T. J. was always affectionate and his touch, usually a hug or arm around her waist, made her feel warm inside.

After the fall drama production had finished its run, Samantha and T. J. continued to hang out after school. They shared many of the same classes and T.J. suggested that they do their homework together. Before long Samantha found herself doing most of the work with T. J. often copying her answers. Meanwhile, their relationship was becoming more physical. Samantha felt she was doing a good job of setting boundaries to keep things from going "too far". She saw nothing wrong with the heavy petting. It felt good to be loved and appreciated.

Just before the Thanksgiving break they were scheduled to take a major history test. T. J. suggested that they develop some hand signals so they could help each other out on the test. When Samantha responded that it was cheating, he got agitated and told her, "If you love me, you'll help me out." She finally relented.

Samantha tried to call her sister, who lived out of state, to get her advice on the cheating issue; but she found it difficult to bring the topic up. Besides, her sister had her own problems trying to make a decision whether to change jobs. They ended up talking more about that issue and Samantha's dilemma was never discussed.

Samantha asked her mom to go out to lunch on the day after Thanksgiving. Her intent was to discuss her relationship with T. J. Samantha knew her mother and dad liked T. J., but as she observed him around them she realized he was acting just like he did when he was on stage. During lunch when Samantha tried to talk about T. J. and his demands her mom replied, "You know, boys will be boys. I used to help your dad out, too." In the end they talked about their travel plans for the Christmas holiday. Samantha began to feel even guiltier about her actions. When she tried to talk to her friends about T. J. they just replied, "We told you so."

Just before the Christmas break T. J. slipped Samantha a note as they were leaving their history class. When she got to her locker she opened it to read that he was asking for some space to see other girls over the break. She confronted him after school with the question, "Does this mean we're breaking up?" His response was, "I still love you. I just think we've gotten too serious."

Samantha spent most of her Christmas break depressed. She felt used. She swore that it would be a long time before she trusted another boy. She was also angry with her parents, especially her mom. They seemed more concerned about having a good time than her personal issues.

Communication has long been an issue for me. In my mind we put too much emphasis on communicating our opinions and not enough on listening to others. We offer high school classes on public speaking, but do we offer similar courses on public listening?

Countless books are written on how to get your point across, but few can be found on the topic of how to understand the needs and feelings of others. We even elect public officials based on their ability to communicate. A slick, articulate speech can swing an election.

In their book *Joined at the Heart: The Transformation of the American Family,* Al and Tipper Gore also address the issue of communication with teens. "Communicating with teenagers has always been difficult. These days it doesn't seem to be getting easier; the list of parental worries has grown much longer as life has gotten much more unpredictable and new challenges have arisen."[1]

Al and Tipper Gore further note:

> As the slow process of asserting their individuality and independence continues, and as friends and peers begin to occupy most of their free hours, teens seem to resent the kind of instruction and guidance that they accepted unconditionally as young children. So, pressured by the demands of work, many parents succumb to the temptation of leaving well enough alone and sharply reduce their efforts to communicate with their teens.[2]

We are a society that struggles to listen to each other. Families can spend an entire week on vacation together and never get beyond the "small talk stage" to the real issues in their lives. A couple can be married for years and never have real honest, intimate conversation. We can work with someone for years and not really know them as a person. We are a society where people greet each other with a casual, "How's it going?" but we cringe when somebody actually starts to tell us. Quite frankly we think, "I care about you, but I really don't care to the point where I want to get involved in your life."

As parents most of us sincerely love our kids and want to help them get through the difficult teen years. Positive parent/child communication is a key component in this process. A good portion of that communication involves listening to our kids.

The Search Institute is a respected organization when it comes to helping parents and those who relate to teens work together to establish a nurturing and caring environment. Search Institute has identified forty assets that healthy teens need to possess. Two of the external assets relate to the relationship between the parent and the teen. Sixty-eight percent of teens reported feeling supported by their parents (Asset 1) but only twenty-eight percent indicate that the communication with their parents is positive (Asset 2).[3] The reality is parents may be communicating, but may not be communicating in a manner that nurtures the relationship with their teen. Even parents who do a good job of establishing and enforcing boundaries might not be effective in communicating the reasons behind them. In the process, the teens end up feeling belittled, and their self esteem is lowered.

Most teenagers desire a positive relationship with their parents. The study "Parents Make a Difference," a program of the University of Wisconsin Extension, confirms this. In identifying things teens worry about, getting along with parents (seventy-five percent) is second only to getting good grades (ninety-six percent). The study also posed the question, "If you were having a personal problem and needed someone to talk to, who would you most likely go to?"

While friends were first (fifty percent of females and forty percent of males), parents were the second choice (eighteen percent of females and twenty-four percent of males).[4]

In the case of Samantha, she approached her sister first and then her mom. Samantha was facing a difficult decision. Her values were being challenged. She sincerely wanted some advice in dealing with the issue. The communication she longed for wasn't there. If parents long for it and teenagers deeply desire it, the question is: How can open and honest communication be established?

Win-Win Communication

Win-Win Communication is a conversation where all participants feel that they have both been heard and respected. "Teens want to be understood and parents want to be heard, though win-win communication is not always evident," notes *Family Works*, a newsletter published by the University of Illinois Extension. "Each participant really wants to do the best job they can with what they have. In order to make any changes in ourselves, we need other people or supportive relationships in our lives."[4]

Dr. Tom Gordon, the founder of Parent Effectiveness Training (PET), is usually credited with the concept of "Win-Win Communication." I was first exposed to PET in the mid-seventies. I went through the training myself and went on to be a workshop leader. A key component in "Win-Win Communication" is unconditional acceptance. "When people are able to feel and communicate genuine acceptance of another, they possess a capacity for being an effective helping agent for the other."[5]

A FAILURE TO COMMUNICATE

Communication where all participants feel both loved and accepted should be everyone's goal. It especially should be the objective for parents who love their children and have their welfare and safety at heart. This kind of communication doesn't just happen. It takes effort. It begins, however, when we communicate our feelings and listen to and accept the feelings of others.

Communicating Feelings

Communication takes place on various levels.

Level One: Facts

Surface communication deals with facts

Your teen comes home and reports, "It's really raining outside."

Level Two: Response

Responds to what others have said

You reply, "I heard the weather report and it's going to rain all night."

Level Three: Opinions and Judgments

Offers perspective

Your teen responds, "You spend too much time worrying about the weather."

Level Four: Share Feelings

We open ourselves to others

You respond, "I get concerned when you are driving on wet roads."

Level Five: Share Inner Thoughts

We share ourselves

You continue, "The thought of something happening to you scares me. I am not sure I could handle having you get seriously hurt or killed."

Through the above process you have shared your feelings and also given your teen the permission to share, as well. As a result we have become real and authentic to the person with whom we are communicating. There are risks when we've exposed our inner feelings and made ourselves vulnerable. But this kind of authentic conversation between teens and adults is vital.

In Samantha's case, she gave many indications that she wanted to talk to someone about both her feelings and her predicament. No one listened. The conversation never advanced beyond the most basic level.

Watch for Signs and Cues

Let's go back to Samantha's story. She was giving her family signs that something was wrong. She is also the one who initiated the lunch with her mom. Just suppose that instead of the placating comment, "Boys will be boys," her mom had responded with the question, "Are you being pressured to do something you don't feel comfortable with?" The door would be open for Samantha to talk about her problem. "Yes, T. J. wants me to help him cheat on a test."

When I was working as a school counselor I tried to be in the hallway during passing periods. Sometimes I would stand outside my office door but other times I would find another spot to observe students. When a student who was always friendly and outgoing suddenly seemed sullen and withdrawn, it was usually a tip-off that something was amiss. Students also tend to move about in groups, hanging out with the same group of friends. A change in that routine could also be an indication that there is a problem.

A FAILURE TO COMMUNICATE

Parents need to be observing the lives on their kids and their peers in the same way. It gives us the opportunity to report what we are observing and express our concern. That opens the door, should there be an issue. Often students who are dealing with personal issues feel isolated, as if no one cares. Our inquiry provides the opportunity to talk about it. Even if they are not at that point, we have showed we care about them.

Just because the issue comes to the surface doesn't mean it's going to be dealt with. If our initial response is to placate the person's feelings like Samantha's mom did with her, "boys will be boys" response, we have defeated the purpose. Worse yet is when the person is belittled, with a comment such as, "You should be happy a boy has shown interest in you."

Jumping to Conclusions

Difficulty communicating often leads to another mistake that parents make: jumping to conclusions. Samantha's mom might immediately conclude she is a willing participant in the ploy. What Samantha really is looking for is help in how to deal with a situation where she is being asked to do something that goes against her values.

Let's say your daughter comes in after being out late with her boyfriend on a Friday night. You happen to be up waiting in the living room when she walks in all starry-eyed from her night with "Mr. Wonderful." She sits down in the chair, takes a deep breath and says, "Sometimes I wish I could marry him right now."

A mom's first response might be, "I don't even want you thinking about getting married until you are done with college." A dad's response might be a vision of walking his little girl down the aisle followed by, "I am not ready for this."

Both have jumped to the conclusion that their daughter is contemplating doing something she might regret. Your daughter might just be letting you know she is infatuated with her boyfriend, or that she is experiencing the warm feelings of being in love. Actually, getting married to him at this point in time is not even being considered.

In this case your positive response might open the door to a discussion on love and the feelings that go with it. An appropriate response might be, "It sounds to me like you are in love." Teens will often make outlandish statements to either open the door to a discussion or just to get your reaction. If you have brought your daughter up to make good choices with regard to relationships, she probably knows marriage is not something to be entered into casually.

Developing an Action Plan

Communication is a necessity in our world. We rely on communication to help us make others aware of our needs. We count on communication to help us facilitate activities we are involved in. Communication allows us to manage our lives. When it comes to families, especially those with teenagers, we need to use communication to get to the heart of their lives. That means listening for feelings. Communication also becomes the vehicle through which we begin to get a glimpse of their world.

A FAILURE TO COMMUNICATE

Let's get back to Samantha. Her parents had done a good job of instilling values. She was able to take a stand in terms of how physical T. J. got. She also felt guilty over having helped T. J. cheat. It would have been helpful to have someone affirm her decisions and encourage her. Samantha's story also provides the opportunity to talk about teens and their emotions. Samantha's relationship with T. J. introduced her to a whole new set of feelings. She was experiencing intimacy with a boy for the first time and it felt good. But remember what we learned in the first chapter about the teenage brain. Someone needed to talk to her about her emotions and the fact that she might sometimes have difficulty processing those feelings.

Make Positive Communication a Priority

Communication doesn't just happen, especially if we have a track record of not listening. If we have open and honest communication with our kids beginning with the toddler stage, the transition to the teen years should move smoothly. If that is not the case, it is never too late to start. Just realize it is a long process to regain trust and establish openness. Adults in theory should be more mature, therefore communication should start with us. Be honest with your teens about your own struggles, needs and feelings. Yes, that does make you vulnerable and they could take advantage of that, but it's worth the risk. If you love them unconditionally, something God requires of us as parents and models so well for us, you might find some of the most honest and meaningful conversation takes place in the late teen and adult years. Be patient.

Listen and Watch for Cues

Changes in mood, in friends, or in routine could be signals that you should be extra alert to what is happening with your teenager. This doesn't mean you have to intervene or even ask, "What's going on?" Rather, it indicates that something might be going on. It means that our antennae need to be up, waiting for opportunities to open the door. Be ready to listen when your teen is ready to talk

BE WILLING TO INVEST TIME ON THEIR TERMS

Approaching our teens when they come home from school or when they are in the middle of a project is generally not a good idea. Just like the rest of us, they need to be in the mood to talk. Late night, after homework is done might be a good time to check in with them and ask how they are doing. Long drives in the car might also provide the opportunity. A one on one meal out could also prove to be fertile ground for meaningful conversation.

BE PATIENT

Establishing open and honest communication takes time. If you've struggled communicating with your child before, it's not going to change overnight. It is however, up to you to open the door. Your openness and expressions of unconditional love are the key ingredients in moving toward a loving and open relationship. Even if you've had a good relationship with your child in the past, you may find the teen years a challenge. Anticipate that and acknowledge that the changes are part of the maturing process as your teen grows in independence. My experience with my own children tells me the deepest, most intimate conversations happened as they grew older and moved out on their own. It may seem difficult, but patiently continuing to work on your relationship may still see results down the road.

NOTES

1. Al and Tipper Gore, *Joined at the Heart: The Transformation of the American Family* (New York: Henry Holt and Company, 2002), 99.
2. Ibid., 100.
3. www.search-institute.org/research/assets/assetfreqs.html
4. www.uwex.edu/ces/cty/grant/tap/parentresources.html
5. www.urbanext.uiuc.edu/familyworks/teen-04.html
6. www.gordontraining.com/the-power-of-the-language-of-acceptance

4

Mistake #3: Not Providing a Support System

Like many contemporary families, Joan and Hank lived over a thousand miles from their closest relatives. They both had roots in the Midwest, but Hank had taken a job in the South fifteen years ago and they had settled in. He had changed jobs a couple of times and they had moved to a new home in the suburbs. Although they weren't "born and bred," they now considered themselves southerners. They had trips north every year to see family, but the holidays were usually spent at home with an annual trip to Colorado to ski.

Both Joan and Hank had careers. Zack was their only child, born when both were in their early thirties. They felt blessed when he arrived and really tried to be good parents. They had a small group of friends, mostly business associates and other couples from their church. They did tend to socialize most weekends, usually leaving Zack with a teenage babysitter.

Zack grew up a normal child. He was a good student and never seemed to be a discipline problem at school. Zack was involved in sports, playing both little league baseball and youth soccer. When he entered middle school he decided to focus on baseball. His middle school coach suggested that he play on a select summer team if his parents were serious about him playing high school baseball. The coach of the team had a great reputation for producing winning teams and several of his former players had gone on to be successful at both the high school and college level. They often saw the coach yell at players, but passed it off as his competitive nature. Halfway through his second season on the team, Zack informed his parents he wanted to quit. He stated that baseball wasn't fun anymore. As a result, Zack entered high school with no real extra-curricular interest. He did have a few good friends from the neighborhood. They were basically good kids who enjoyed playing video games and hanging out together on the weekends.

Even though they lived in the suburbs, Zack and his parents had maintained their membership in a church in their former neighborhood in the city. Most of the other church members also lived in the suburbs, but they enjoyed the fellowship. They considered the pastor a good friend. Zack was one of only eight teenagers in the church and he felt little connection with any of them since they all went to different schools. There was no youth group to speak of. Joan and Hank insisted that Zack go to the youth Bible class while they went to the adult class led by the pastor, but Zack told them the class was boring. In the end they decided to go out for brunch on Sundays after services rather than attend Bible class.

A whole new world opened up for Zack when he turned sixteen. All of his friends got their drivers licenses, and Zack went through driver education, as well. Shortly after, his parents bought him a car of his own. It was used, but its racy looks fit his image. Within six months Zack had gotten two tickets for speeding. With the second he also was cited for a curfew violation, which meant he had to appear before a judge. His parents took away his car keys as a result. He now had to rely on his friends for transportation.

Joan and Hank were out with friends one Saturday night when they got a call from the police that Zack had been taken to the emergency room after being involved in an accident. When they got to the hospital they found Zack was not injured, but the police informed them that alcohol had been involved. When they got home they tried to talk with Zack about what had taken place, but he stated his life was none of their business. Joan and Hank were at a loss as to where to turn for help in dealing with their son.

Like many in my generation I grew up surrounded by relatives. My mother's parents lived three blocks away, and five other aunts and uncles lived within a mile. In addition, I had Sunday school teachers, youth counselors, and other adults I related to on a regular basis at church. This is not the case for many teens today. For my own kids, their grandparents were voices on the phone and aunts and uncles were the people we visited on vacation.

In the previous chapter we talked about the struggle that parents have establishing meaningful relationships with their teens. If communication is a problem between parents and teens, it is even worse between teens and other adults. Search Institute reports that only forty-three percent of teens report feeling supported by other adults.[1]

In his book, *Hurt: Inside the World of Today's Teenagers*, Chap Clark talks about the sub-culture that today's teens have established to isolate and protect themselves from the adult world. Clark reports that teens feel abandoned by adults. He observes, "Adolescents have suffered the loss of safe relationships and intimate settings that serve as the primary nurturing for those traveling the path from child to adult."[2]

Clark goes on to say that the loss of meaningful adult relationships is the most devastating thing that has happened to teens. He further notes: "Whether it is a coach, a school teacher, a parent, music teacher or a Sunday school counselor, mid-adolescents intuitively believe that nearly every adult they have encountered has been subtly out to get something from them."[3]

The University of Illinois – Chicago has established a center for teen mentoring focused on working with urban youth. They have determined that the after school setting provides an excellent opportunity for the development of informal mentoring relationships. Teachers and staff people provide a support system for teens while helping them with their homework, instructing them on life skills and offering recreation opportunities. In many cases those staffing these urban mentoring programs are adults who live in the same communities they serve. As a result they are in a position to connect with teens and offer advice and guidance. Especially in an urban setting, mentoring makes a difference.[4]

Further research by UIC reveals that teens that have adult mentors have:

- a greater likelihood of completing high school and attending college,
- a decreased likelihood of being in a gang,

- a higher self esteem,
- a greater level of physical activity, as well as
- a regular use of birth control.[5]

The need for mentoring urban youth may seem obvious. But my experience is that families who live outside of an urban environment often get lulled into a false sense of security. The tree-lined streets, well kept lawns and low crime rates lead them to believe their world is a safe place to raise their kids. They can fill their lives with activities that keep them and their kids involved. The danger is they can become so active they don't see the reality. Today's teens often do not have meaningful relationships with adults. Suburban teens need mentors just as much as those who live in urban environments. Parents need to make sure they and their teens have a support system.

In the case of Zack, who we met at the beginning of this chapter, there were no significant adult role models in his life. The three usual sources for such relationships are: 1) extended family 2) extracurricular activities 3) religious or community organizations. Because of the location of the family, there was no extended family close by. Zack was involved in baseball, but an overbearing coach seemed to have soured him on that experience. Zack was not connected with anyone at his church and was not involved in any other extra-curricular organization. Other than his father, Zack had no adult men in his life who served as role models. There was no support system for him and his parents.

Adult Mentors

It is easy to get the terms role model and mentor confused. Both play important roles, especially in the lives of teenagers who are struggling to find the right path to adulthood. Role models are individuals whose patterns of behavior influence those around them. It is always the hope that parents are good role models.

The concept of mentoring can be traced back to Greek mythology. Mentor was a faithful friend to Ulysses. He was the teacher and advisor to Ulysses' son while he was away fighting the Trojan War. Today we define a mentor as a wise and trusted counselor.[6] Mentors can be found in a variety of roles: teachers, coaches, youth counselors and scout leaders. Mentoring is a two-way relationship. One must be in the position to teach and counsel, but must also be perceived as caring, loving and accepting.

When it comes to working with teens, what characteristics make a person a good mentor? My experience is that good mentors of teens have the following characteristics.

Mentors are good listeners. People often ask me, "What does it take to be a good counselor?" My response is always the same, "You need to start by being a non-judgmental listener."

During my years as a school counselor it was almost a daily occurrence for me to have a student come into my office agitated and angry, then leave ten to fifteen minutes later calm. In between he or she did ninety-five percent of the talking. Along the way a lot of emotion was expressed, usually anger and frustration. I could never allow myself to take what was said personally or to be offended by language or opinions that were vented. I wanted my office to be seen as a safe place to let off steam and express what was going on. It was better for students to say it to me than to act it out in the hallway or parking lot in ways that could cause trouble or even be dangerous.

Teens need someone with whom they can share their thoughts and feelings. I have come to realize that teens don't want someone who will give them advice. Instead, they are seeking someone who will help them sort through their feelings and help them analyze the situation.

Mentors are forgiving. In my years of working with teens I have had my heart broken countless times. It is a given that teenagers, like people of any age, are sometimes going to let you down. I also know that as a sinner, I have made poor choices that have disappointed those who trusted me. In some cases I have hurt a student by something I said or did. If I admit and take ownership of my mistake I expect to be forgiven. In working with teens I must practice the same principle.

Forgiveness doesn't mean a lack of accountability for actions. Poor choices have consequences. Sometimes the consequence is the natural result of the action, other times it may involve a logical imposed consequence. It is also important to communicate our feelings of hurt and disappointment in a non-judgmental way. Teens need to understand that sometimes their actions result in a need to rebuild trust.

Mentors are interested in the world teens live in. I enjoy almost all types of music. There are two exceptions: opera and rap. A good friend and humanities teacher, Steve Lund, has offered to enlighten me on the former. He's convinced, and I can see his point, that my disdain for opera is because I've never tried to understand it. When it comes to rap, however, I have learned to tolerate and even enjoy it at times. That's because rap is part of the youth culture. Even "lily-white" teens from the suburb listen to and enjoy the urban sound of rap music. Those who want to mentor youth must do their best to understand the culture of youth.

That does not mean we need to become part of or adopt that culture. Jesus told his disciples he wanted them to be "in the world, not of the world." When adults, especially those over the age of forty, try to copy the styles, trends and culture of youth, it can turn kids off. Seeking to learn about and understand their culture shows we are interested in them and the world they live in. Effective mentors can try to respect and understand the culture of youth without trying to "be a kid" again.

Mentors are not self-serving. All three of our children were involved in youth athletics at one point or another. Sometimes I was the coach, but at other times we turned that responsibility over to other adults. My wife and I quickly were able to discern which adults were having a positive impact and which were having a negative impact on our own kids. When you ask most adults who work with children and youth where their motivation lies, they will probably tell you, "I am in this for the kids." The question is do their actions reflect that? A coach or teacher who places unrealistic expectations or pressure on kids probably has another agenda. It is only through observation that you can discern what their true motives are. If the motives are at all suspect, there is a need to meet with the coach or teacher. The issue needs to be confronted. Our teen's long-term welfare might be at stake.

NOT PROVIDING A SUPPORT SYSTEM

While the usual focus is on athletic coaches, the problem can extend to other areas, as well. Sunday school or Bible class teachers whose primary objective is to preserve the church's tradition rather than to nurture faith can potentially have a negative impact. That is especially the case if our desire as parents is the spiritual development of the child. The same can be said for teachers who only view their position as a way to make a living, rather than to impart knowledge and have a positive influence.

Developing an Action Plan

Parents need to develop a support system for their kids. Potential mentors could be coaches, teachers, scout leaders, church youth leaders, or neighbors. Extended family, aunts, uncles, and grandparents can also be mentors.

PLACE YOUR TEENS IN THE RIGHT ENVIRONMENT

Mentoring relationships have to happen naturally and cannot be forced. It's not a formal process like interviewing a new employee. Rather, we need to be intentional in placing our kids in environments where they have contact with caring, open, and loving adults. While we can arrange for the settings and encourage participation, our teens will select those with whom they want a close relationship. Sometimes it's a common interest, other times it's because their personalities mesh, but always it's a matter of finding someone they can trust. Such individuals accept them for who they are.

From my perspective, Zack's downward spiral began when he quit baseball. His comments that, "Baseball isn't fun anymore," should have been a door to talk about his feelings. I suspect what Zack really wanted was to be put in a more nurturing environment. By helping him to process those emotions his parents could have helped him make the decision to continue his baseball career under a different coach rather than giving up the sport. The keys to communicating feelings outlined previously would have helped. If our teens can be open and honest with us, they will be better able to maintain those same patterns with the other significant adults in their lives.

MONITOR AND SUPPORT YOUR TEEN'S INVOLVEMENT

Parents not only need to attend activities their teens are involved in, but should also get to know the adults leading them. Watch the way the adults interact with teens, especially the respect they show teens and the way teens respect them. Monitor your teen's mood after spending time with the adult. Was the time spent with the mentor relaxing and positive? Watch for warning signs that might indicate the adult leader is having a negative impact on teens. Make judgments based on your experiences, not based on what other parents are saying.

TRUST THE MENTOR

A word of warning: If your teens do find an adult they can trust you might sometimes feel left out. It is not uncommon for teens to grow close to significant adults in their lives, especially during times when they are struggling. At such times those adults might be the sounding boards and safe places they need. In a counseling relationship I have often grown close to kids. At such times they often shared things about themselves even their parents did not know. In many cases they didn't want their parents to know because they didn't want them to worry excessively. Once the issue was resolved I strongly encouraged them to talk to their parents about the issue, in some cases becoming an advocate and sitting in on the conversation. If the relationship between you and your teen is healthy and strong they will always gravitate back to you when the issue is resolved.

Being the parent of a teenager can be a lonely experience. Remember, though, that there are other adults who want to help and support you in that effort. Try to be secure enough to accept their help for the benefit of your children.

NOTES

1. www.search-institute.org/research/assets/assetfreqs.html
2. Chap Clark, *Hurt: Inside the World of Today's* Teenagers (Grand Rapids: Baker Academics, 2004), 50.
3. Ibid., 50.
4. www.mentoring.org
5. www.mentoring.org
6. http://dictionary.reference.com

5

Mistake #4: Living Our Dreams Vicariously through Our Kids

Tammy was the daughter of Teresa, a single mom. From the time Tammy was a baby, people were drawn to her enchanting looks. At first Teresa was embarrassed when people stopped her in the supermarket to gaze at her daughter's almost China doll-like face. As Tammy grew into preschool age her golden blond hair only enhanced her beauty.

It was a total stranger at the mall who first planted the seed in Teresa's mind. "Your daughter looks like one of those models in the magazines," the woman commented. "Her looks have to be worth millions," she continued.

Teresa's mind immediately flashed back to her own youth. A high school cheerleader, she had also taken modeling classes. In the end she finally chose cheerleading as her primary focus in high school and college. Her dream of being a professional model dimmed as she faced the reality of finishing college and starting a career in real estate. When her marriage to her college sweetheart fell apart after four years, she was left to support herself and her infant daughter. Teresa became a successful real estate agent. She and Tammy lived a comfortable lifestyle. Teresa had the financial resources to send Tammy to modeling classes, and by the time she was in third grade she was regularly missing school to attend photo sessions. When the school started to balk at the amount of school Tammy was missing, Teresa looked for a private school that was more accommodating. By this time Tammy was working with a modeling agency that was able to help them search for a "nurturing environment" for a potential super-model.

Tammy entered her first beauty pageant at age eight. Tammy's singing voice was barely average, but over time her voice matured with the help of private lessons. Singing became her talent on stage. By the time Tammy reached high school she was competing in teen pageants regularly, often finishing near the top. While modeling opportunities continued, there was more competition for the most lucrative sessions. Her mother encouraged her and reminded her, "Your career could be our future."

Tammy couldn't help feeling pressured to keep a trim figure. She did a good job hiding her eating disorder. At home she ate small portions. She told her mom she was dieting, but often purged afterwards. She usually ended up throwing away the hot lunch served at school. When the school counselor noticed that Tammy was disturbingly thin, she insisted that she eat. That caused Tammy to purge in the school bathroom. When the counselor discovered Tammy's habit she called her mom. The counselor recommended both a complete physical and counseling. Tammy's doctor referred them to a cardiologist who discovered that two heart valves were leaking. Tammy's dream of being a super-model was put on hold as she was sent to an adolescent treatment program that specialized in eating disorders.

LIVING OUR DREAMS VICARIOUSLY...

✧

I made a casual observation during a recent walk through the park near our home.

Attendance at youth baseball games peaks at the tee-ball level. Parents, grandparents, aunts, uncles and older siblings surrounded the field where the youngest players played. Some were barely able to hold the bat much less swing it, and spent more time watching the dandelions grow than the opposing hitter. On an adjacent field where eleven and twelve year-old little leaguers played, the bleachers were half full.

This phenomenon is not limited to the baseball diamond. During the fall I have observed a sideline full of parents watching seven and eight year-olds on the soccer and football fields. The parents are not there to watch a game, rather the practice. They cheer, yell words of encouragement, and yes, often critique the coaches.

We encouraged all of our children to participate in some form of physical activity. Our oldest son played basketball, the younger one soccer. During our daughter's grade school years she participated in gymnastics. My wife and I were some of the few parents who did not line the gym window (the wise coach banned parents from the gym during practice) watching as their children honed their skills. Again, this was only practice, but it was obvious the parents took great pleasure watching their kids. It was also obvious that expectations were high. Many parents talked about what it would take to move their children to the next level. It was obvious the primary focus was on success, rather than physical fitness.

These attitudes are not restricted to athletics. Music and dance recitals are performed in packed halls with parents videotaping every moment. Many parents picture their child as the next "American Idol" or Hollywood star.

The question must be asked: "Who are these activities for?"

Self-Serving Parents

In the previous chapter we addressed the issue of adults who involve themselves in youth activities for the wrong reason. The issue is not limited to those who volunteer. Parents can also be a big part of the problem. In his book *Hurt*, Chap Clark notes, "Sports are no longer child's play, they are a grown-up dog-eat-dog reality."[1] Activities designed to provide our children with exercise and to teach them skills have become a way for parents to stroke their egos.

Clark further relates what he observed at a pee-wee football game. When it got close to the end, the father of one of the boys who was on the team that was behind commanded his son to strip the ball.

> "If you don't strip the ball you're walking home," he screamed. Sure enough, no one was able to strip the ball, and the team we were rooting for lost another game. The son cried as he approached his father. His father with visible reluctance and more than a hint of sarcasm, told the son, "I guess you can't win them all. Let's get the hell out of here."[2]

This is a lesson I had to learn personally. Our oldest son, Peter, played basketball in high school. He saw a lot of playing time, even starting some games as a sophomore. Early in his junior year he was approached by a college recruiter. I was excited as the vision of my son playing at the next level danced in my head. A basketball scholarship might be his ticket to college. As we visited with the recruiter in our home I sensed Peter did not share my enthusiasm. Later, in private, Peter shared that the thought of spending four to six hours a day in the training room and on the court was a cost he didn't want to pay. Our son wanted to go to college to get an education, not be a full-time athlete. Basketball was, and still is, something he enjoys casually.

I think we become enamored with our teens' accomplishments for two reasons, both self serving. Part of it is economic reasons and part is vicarious pleasure. Big time professional athletes often make millions. As I write this chapter the local sports pages provide a chronicle of the negotiations between the Texas Rangers and their number one draft pick. The point of contention is the signing bonus, which in reality is one hundred thousand dollars in a million dollar plus contract. The major spokesperson in this case is not the player, but his mother.

Our family has been season ticket holders for TCU Horned Frog football for years. Each season we comment on the few seniors who might have the potential to be drafted by NFL teams. Over seventy-five players line the sideline during home games. Most of them were stars on their high school teams. Many of them are on full athletic scholarships. After a typical season, usually less than five are given opportunity to attend an NFL camp, with even fewer getting the opportunity to play professionally.

The reality is that less than ten percent of the young men who sign contracts to play professional baseball will ever make it to the major leagues even for a brief time. That does not prevent parents from looking at their child and seeing a potential superstar, and their ticket to early retirement.

Mid-Life Crisis

Sometimes what is going on in the maturity process of parents can have a profound impact on how they relate to their children. Mid-life crisis is a good example. Mid-life crisis is defined as a difficult, turbulent period of doubts and reappraisal of one's life.[3] It is a normal transition time that roughly parallels the time during which many parents have teenagers in their home. Typically this point in life takes place during the forties.

Erik Erikson is credited with the theory of social development. Erikson has identified life stages that people typically move through. Each stage involves an internal conflict that must be resolved. What is commonly referred to as mid-life crisis falls into the category Erikson calls "Generativity vs. Self-Absorption."

> **Generativity** is an adult's concern for and commitment to promoting the well-being of youth and future generations through involvement in parenting, teaching, mentoring and other creative contributions that aim to leave a positive legacy of the self for the future.[4] It is a complex psychosocial construct that can be expressed through social demands, inner desires, conscious concerns, beliefs, commitments, behavior, and the overall way in which an adult makes sense of his or her own life. Characteristics of a generative adult include themes such

as witnessing suffering (compassion), moral steadfastness and continuity, love, and goals for the future.[5] As a contrast, self-absorbed individuals are primarily concerned with meeting their own needs and desires.

In my experience I have witnessed the merging of these two needs into the drive for vicarious success. Parents desire to pass on their legacy to the next generation, but do it in a manner that satisfies their own needs and desires. The desire is to see their teens succeed in ways that they could not. Their need is to achieve vicarious success through the achievements of their children.

Vicarious Success

Self-Absorption is behind most self-serving parents who need to live out their dream vicariously through their kids. Christie Crowder notes on the *Parenting Teens* website:

> As parents we want the best for our children and of course want them to be all they can be. Unfortunately sometimes what we want for them is exactly... what we want, not necessarily what they want. This usually happens in high school when the dad who never got to be on the football team is hounding his son to try out. Or the mom who got passed over for Homecoming Queen makes it her life's work campaigning for the popularity of her daughter.[6]

I spent a few seasons coaching high school basketball, including two as a varsity coach. My experience is that on the average, parents have much higher expectations for their kids than do the players themselves. As players assess their talent, and that of the team, they can usually foresee their level of participation and success. The parents in the stands often have a different perspective. In their minds their children deserve more playing time and opportunity to show their skills.

When it comes to our teenagers and their extra-curricular activities, we as parents need to check our expectations at the door. We are doing our kids a disservice when we develop unrealistic visions of success. Children need to be allowed to participate in the activities that interest them and allow them to develop the God-given skills that they have. If our aim is to have our kids develop a healthy and realistic self image, it needs to begin with us.

Teen Self Image

So, how do we help our teens develop a healthy and realistic self image? Here are a few guidelines.

Reinforce their feelings. Feelings are real and very much a part of who we are. We need to respect the feelings that others have, even if we do not agree. Never dismiss those feelings or blow them off. Suppose your teen comes home after practice and states, "I guess I am going to have to get used to sitting on the bench." An appropriate response would be, "It sounds to me like you are frustrated with your role on the team." Nothing is served if our response is, "That's okay. I still love you," or "I know how talented you really are."

Don't repeatedly tell them how much potential they have. Teens need to develop a realistic perception of themselves.

They are best served if they are allowed to do that on their own. When we repeatedly tell them how talented they are, we run the risk of stroking their egos. In the process they will develop an unrealistic view of themselves.

Affirm all their gifts. Those who excel usually get the adoration. The newspapers consistently report the leading scorers. The lead in the school drama usually gets the top billing. What about those who play supporting roles? Even more important, how about those who appear to have no role at all? As a counselor I found great joy in watching students who had to work hard just to achieve a passing grade. Every teenager needs to be affirmed. Identify the gifts each possesses and acknowledge them.

Learn to move on. Life is a journey. As such we will move through various chapters. Our families are best served if we celebrate each chapter and then move on in joyful anticipation of the next. Sometimes those changes and transitions happen suddenly, like when serious injury ends a promising career. What about if our daughter (or son) just decides to not go out for the team her (or his) senior year? We need to accept that and respect her (or his) decision.

DEVELOPING AN ACTION PLAN

All parents want their children to grow up to be successful and self-supporting. We also strive to help them develop a healthy and realistic self image. We previously talked about the need to develop a support system for our kids. We want to surround them with adults who are good role models. It must begin with us, however. We must have healthy and realistic views of ourselves.

PARENTING WITHOUT GUILT

LET GO OF YOUR DREAMS

This also involves letting go of our own dreams and looking to the future. Parents must constantly be examining their motives when it comes to the lives of their children. That means having healthy perspective ourselves, as well. We must have a healthy sense of who we are and where we are headed.

When it comes to the activities our teens involve themselves in we need to ask, "Who are they doing this for?" Is it something they choose to do, or something that we need them to do? Listen to and encourage their dreams instead of imposing yours on them.

HELP YOUR TEEN DEVELOP A VISION FOR THE FUTURE

One of my greatest joys as a high school counselor was helping students cast visions for their futures. During the first semester each year, I would teach a careers class with all juniors as my students. Together we would discover what their gifts and interests were. Then we would explore career opportunities using those gifts and post-high school options for them. I sincerely believe it made a difference. Many of them approached both their studies and their college planning with a new sense of purpose.

As your children enter the teen years, sit down with them and work through a similar process. Discuss their long-term goals and help them develop a plan to get there. In the previous chapter we discussed the concept of mentoring. One possibility is to use your network of friends to identify individuals who are in the career your teens are interested in. Is it possible those people could become mentors to your teens? Even if they are not in a position to mentor, they might be open to discussing their jobs with your son or daughter.

Some form of physical activity, whether organized or done casually, needs to be included in a teen's schedule. In addition, he or she might choose to participate in other extracurricular activities. Part of the maturation process should be learning to balance all the activities. Those management skills will become invaluable in the future.

Let Them Go

It is your child's future, not yours. Your child needs to set the goals and make the decisions on how to get there. Part of the maturation process is learning from experience. Being given the opportunity to succeed or fail can teach important life lessons that are better learned before venturing into the cold, hard world.

NOTES

1. Chap Clark, *Hurt: Inside the World of Today's Teenagers* (Grand Rapids: Baker Academics, 2004), 114.
2. Ibid., 115.
3. R.L. Gould, *Transformations: Growth and Changes in Adult Life* (New York: Simon and Schuster, 1978).
4. www.seap.northwestern.edu/foley/research
5. Ibid.
6. www.parentingteens.com, Are You Living Vicariously Through Your Teen?

6

Mistake #5: Being a Manager Rather than a Consultant

Ted was the younger son of Jon and Meg. Both his parents had graduated from the same major state university. Jon had gone on to earn his M. B. A. Their older son Tim was attending their alma mater. They had the same expectations for Ted.

Unlike his older brother, Ted seemed to lack both motivation and direction. His grades were okay, but he invested little time in academics, choosing instead to read science fiction books and play video games. While Tim had worked on the yearbook and been a member of both the cross country and track teams in high school, Ted showed no interest in extra-curricular activities. At his parent's strong encouragement, he had gotten a job at a local grocery store when he turned sixteen. They hoped it would teach him some responsibility.

From their experience with Tim, they knew the college admissions process. They had planned financially for the post-high school education of both boys. Ted had told them he was not interested in college and mentioned enlisting in the Navy as a possibility after graduation. Both of his parents expressed displeasure with that plan. "Whether it's our alma mater or another school, the expectation is that you will attend a college," they stated.

When Ted's PSAT scores arrived in the late fall of his junior year, it only reinforced his parents' opinion that he was underachieving. His score was even higher than Tim's. When his mother mentioned his score was his "ticket to the school of his choice," Ted got agitated. "It's my future," he muttered as he closed the door to his room.

When the college brochures started arriving in the mail, Ted either ignored them or tossed them in the trash. His mom managed to save some of them and kept a file on schools she thought might interest him. When she discussed the situation with Jon, he suggested they take a couple of days in February and take Ted on a tour of two or three schools, including their alma mater. "Maybe once he gets on a campus his feelings will change," he stated. When they mentioned the plan to Ted he balked, but finally relented when they reminded him he would be missing two days of school. They even offered to let him pick the hotels where they stayed. When they returned Ted expressed that he was not excited about any of the schools they visited. He finally agreed to apply to one of the schools just to placate his parents.

Ted worked full-time at the grocery store during the summer prior to his senior year. After a month he got promoted from being a bagger to working in the produce section. At the end of the summer he informed his parents that his plans had changed. The store manager had offered him a full-time position in the produce department following graduation. "I don't want my son spending the rest of his life working in a supermarket," his dad yelled when informed of his plan. "I want you to have the same opportunity your brother had."

In the fall Ted reluctantly completed the application to one college. He promised to have the school counselor send in his transcript and recommendation. Shortly before Thanksgiving, Meg found the completed application buried underneath a stack of papers in his room. Noting that the deadline was fast approaching, she called the high school to talk to the counselor. In doing so, she discovered that Ted had done nothing toward completing the application process. She requested that the needed information be sent to the college. The next day she put the application in a file folder and made the four hour round trip to the college. She hand delivered the application to the admissions office.

When she informed Ted what she had done, he went ballistic, shouting, "I wish you would stay out of my life." Two weeks later the rejection letter from the college came in the mail. Ted seemed relieved at the news.

Consultants

"A consultant (from the Latin *consultare* meaning "to discuss" from which we derive words such as *consul and counsel*) is a professional who provides advice in a particular area of expertise..."1

There is a considerable difference between being an expert and being a consultant. While both an expert and a consultant could be valuable resources and are in the position to offer advice, the similarity ends there. Experts offer advice based on their experience. Consultants offer their expertise based on the situation and goals of their client. We can further say that consultants:

- only go where they are invited,
- learn about the client and his or her situation,
- have information and expertise relevant to that situation,
- give information and then step back.

We can also state that consultants don't:

- go where they are not invited,
- give advice based on their experience or situation,
- keep reminding their clients of their wise counsel.

Moving From Being a Manager to Being a Consultant

As parents we can become very proficient at managing our kids' lives. That comes out of necessity. Infants and toddlers cannot do much for themselves. As a result we strive to meet their every need and to create an environment that keeps them safe. As they grow we learn to oversee their lives. We schedule their activities, provide them with the resources to participate in those activities, and even provide the transportation. But somewhere along the line that role begins to change.

If our ultimate goal is to raise children to be independent, self-confident adults, we must equip them to manage their own lives. While it's a gradual process, a major part of the growth happens during the teen years.

Take, for example, the issue of clothing. In the early years we probably selected the clothes and even dressed our kids. During the elementary years we might have helped them select what they wore for various occasions, but allowed them to dress themselves. We still had some control because, for the most part, we bought what they wore. As they entered middle school we might have allowed them to select their own clothes. By their high school years they probably wanted to do some of their own shopping, in time even using their own financial resources to do the purchasing.

The issue, however, becomes how to prepare them to make good choices about what they wear. The selection and style of clothes is probably one of the major points of conflict between parents and teens. What happens when we can no longer manage what our kids buy and wear?

Giving advice, when it comes to apparel, is the easy part. Getting our teens to take that advice might be impossible. In fact, in some cases our advice might be the motivation to do the exact opposite.

So how should a parent give advice? According to the website "Growing up Matters", you don't. It states, "Now at a first glance this probably sounds ridiculous. After all, parents have more experience of life and most would agree that a parent's job is to pass on that experience to their children. The problem is that advice is really just a way of maintaining control."[2]

When we try to steer our teens toward making decisions based on our perspective or needs we really are managing their lives. It is worse yet when we make decisions for them. It's a way of maintaining control. It breeds rebellion. What's going to happen when they are beyond our influence?

In the case of Ted, the young man we met at the beginning of this chapter, few would argue with the advice his parents gave him.

They advised him to get a job and he did that. As a result he began to think in terms of a post-high school job working in the grocery business. He had taken their advice, but it did not have the result they had planned. In this case their advice (strong encouragement) was an attempt to manage his life. Their real objective was to have Ted see the value of a college education. When that failed, they developed a plan to steer him into making the decision they wanted. They attempted to manage his life. Not only did they fail in that attempt, but they severely damaged their relationship with him in the process.

As a school counselor I witnessed many parents who tried to manage their students onto a future path. Sometimes they were successful and things worked out. More often, however, the student followed the path but resented it or, worse yet, failed because they felt no investment in the decision. It may have worked out better if the parents had recognized the need to transition from the role of being a manager of their child's life to the role of being a consultant.

How to Be a Consultant to Your Teen

Seek permission. Always ask your teen if they want your advice before you give it. If they say "yes," then you have their permission. If the answer is "no," respect that as well. If they venture out on their own and fail, perhaps next time they might be more willing to listen to your perspective. If they try it their way and find success, even to the smallest degree, they have learned to be more independent.

Ask probing questions. As a parent you do have the right to ask questions, in the same way your child might question you. If they ask you a question such as, "Why is it so important that I go to youth group at church?" they deserve an honest answer that demonstrates your concern for them and their needs. You might say, "I value your spiritual growth just as much as I do your academic growth." An unacceptable response is, "Your mother and I went to youth group when we were your age." By asking probing questions you are helping them think through their decisions. In so doing you are helping them think through their decisions. You are also gaining insights into their world. If the issue is their lack of involvement in your church's youth ministry a probing question might be, "What exactly don't you like about the youth group?" or "What are you looking for in a church youth group?" You are going to gain more insight through asking probing questions than just asking, "Why don't you want to go to youth group?" Probing questions must be asked in a non-judgmental way in order not to belittle your kids and their thoughts and feelings. Information gained becomes helpful as you shift into your consulting role. Remember, consultants learn about their client's situation and offer information relative to it.

Even if they refuse your advice, you still have the right to ask specific questions: What do you hope to accomplish through this? Is this going to help you get where you ultimately want to be? Have you thought how this might affect others?

Be a resource. Part of being a parent is providing our kids with the information they need to be successful. Some of this information should come directly from us, but some will come from outside sources. This involves anticipating when the issues requiring extra information might arise. For example, go over your expectations for proper and improper behavior when on a date. Remind them of your parental responsibility. Tell them you expect a phone call if their plans change or they run into a problem.

Make sure your teens have the information needed to make the right choices on all kinds of decisions: drugs, alcohol, sex, and selecting the right college to name a few. Don't preach. Don't threaten. Just provide information.

Back off. If you work with a consultant, you don't expect them to call you every other day asking if you are taking their advice. They might check in with you periodically for follow-up, but what you do with the information they provide is up to you. The same thing applies to working with our teens. Let them know how you feel and then let them decide. Ultimately the decision has to be theirs. They have to take ownership.

Commend them when they do well. Don't lavish the praise, but do let them know when you are proud or appreciate what they have done. Focus on their strengths, not their weaknesses. Be patient and allow them to discover their own shortcomings.

Listen but don't judge. Teenagers often think out loud. They might only be revealing their thought process by what they are saying. Listen to them and report what you hear them saying in a non-judgmental way. *Don't immediately jump to conclusions.* Rather, use probing questions to determine what they are really thinking.

Life as a Consultant

Dr. Michael Riera has not only survived high school, but has come back time and time again attempting to understand teenagers and their world. His book *Surviving School,* helps teens by providing insights on key issues they grapple with. Some of his thoughts are good advice for parents to hear, as well.

BEING A MANAGER RATHER THAN A CONSULTANT

Dr. Riera tells parents to embrace estrangement. "The development of personal identity during adolescence includes moving away from, but not becoming disconnected from family. Your teenager needs to show himself that he doesn't need you."[3] As part of that process parents can expect to be fired as managers and rehired as consultants, Dr. Riera notes.

The advice from Dr. Riera and others might be difficult for parents to hear. After all, we love our kids and the thought of being alienated from them, even for a short period, is difficult to accept. Life is a journey and all relationships go through changes. We want our teens to arrive at their destinations successfully, feeling good about themselves and their relationships with us.

Developing an Action Plan

We recognize that our teenagers are changing and so is our relationship with them. They might not always follow the paths we want them to take, but if we provide them with a loving environment, the resources they need to survive, and freedom to try, we might be surprised at the results. This puts added pressure on us as parents now. The value system that we instill and principles that we base our lives on will serve as the framework our children carry into the future. Rules are not enough. Any boundaries, along with the consequences for the same, must be accompanied by an explanation as to why we feel they are important.

One way to help ourselves accomplish this is to project what we would like our lives to be like in the future. Picture the way you would like things to be in ten to twelve years. Obviously, one thing we hope for is our children's independence. Perhaps they are married with children of their own, living in a house they are buying. It is the hope that they have a career where they feel happy and successful. The key word here is "happy." Happiness can never be defined from our perspective. Also keep in mind that everyone matures at a different pace. Some young people will have a clear vision for their future by the age of sixteen, while others will graduate from high school still lacking a sense of direction. Either way, our role should be the same: to support and encourage. If we dedicate ourselves to being the best parents we can be, ultimately God will carry out his plan in the lives of our children, in the same way he does in ours.

NOTES

1. http://en.wikipedia.org/wiki/Consulting
2. www.growingupmatters.com/getting_your_point_across.phtml
3. Surviving High School, http://kidscource.com

7

Mistake #6: Not Letting Go

Cat was the oldest daughter of Char and her stepfather Martin. Char had little contact with her birth father, who lived out of state. Char had married Martin when Cat was in second grade. In time they had three more children, two girls and a boy.

Having raised Cat by herself almost from birth, Char had always been protective of her. Char never left Cat in the care of anyone but close relatives, usually her own mother. When Cat started school, Char found ways to volunteer so that she could be involved in her daughter's life. By the time she graduated from grade school, Char was on a first name basis with the principal. During Cat's final year at the school, Char was named Volunteer of the Year, an award she cherished.

Cat moved on to a large middle school that offered a very different environment. Char had heard rumors of a drug culture at the school and tightly controlled Cat's social life. Cat was invited to a few parties, but when her mom started asking questions and even stopping by the homes during the events, the invitations stopped.

Cat entered high school with few friends and was viewed by most of her classmates as quiet and shy. Her mother wouldn't let her ride the bus to school with the other students from their neighborhood. Instead, she drove her to school and picked her up each day. Cat was not involved in extra-curricular activities. She spent evenings and weekends watching her younger siblings instead.

Cat was a conscientious student who got good grades. During her senior year she had a very demanding English teacher. When Cat received a C+ on an essay that was going to adversely affect her grade, Char called the teacher. When she did not get the response she wanted she went to the Dean of Students, eventually getting the grade changed to a B-.

Cat wanted to be a nurse and was accepted to several colleges with excellent programs. She finally settled on a school an hour from home. She and Char spent the summer before her departure shopping and planning for Cat's college experience. Cat lived in a dorm, but returned home every weekend. Her mom also came every Wednesday night to help her with her laundry. Halfway through the year she had serious roommate issues, but the school would not allow her to move out of the dorm. She managed to make it through the year, but decided to transfer to a community college a mile from home for her sophomore year. The nursing program was not as strong and she was not able to transfer back into the nursing program at the university. In the end she dropped out of college and got a job working as a receptionist in a doctor's office. She continued to live at home.

My wife and I have always believed that we raised our kids to let them go. There has come a point with each of our three children when we knew they were ready to go. From experience I can tell you there is no ride longer and quieter than the trip home after dropping off your child at college. Our son Mark attended a school almost a thousand miles away from home. We wanted each of our children to have the opportunity to pursue their dreams. That did not make it any easier. When our oldest son, Peter, left home for his freshman year at Texas Christian University, I penned the following prayer:

I can see his figure in the rearview mirror,
standing at the curb waving.
I guess that is why his mother stayed home.
Saying goodbye here is difficult.

Lord, I know we've been planning this for a long time.
It's what parenting is all about.
You raise them to let them go.
We all know he is ready to leave.
I have no doubt about his talent or maturity.
He's going to do well.

But it's difficult to let him go.
I know he's going to face failures and disappointments.
He's going to struggle with some things
and make some mistakes.

Lord, I place him into Your hands.
Watch over him and protect him.
Lift him up and forgive him when he falls.
I pray that my relationship with him will
continue to grow while we're apart,
Just as I pray his relationship with you will grow.
Amen.[1]

No matter how ready they are, it's still difficult to let them go. Not only did our youngest son, Mark, choose a school a long way from home, but he wanted to study in Europe for a semester. He was scheduled to go in January 2002, while the world was still recovering from the events of 9-11. Traveling abroad was still a scary proposition. We took a deep breath, said many prayers, and let him go. We really celebrated the day that we heard he was back on American soil. Reflecting back, the four months he spent studying and traveling abroad changed him and shaped him more than any other time in his educational experience. Mark learned how to live on his own in a foreign country. He also learned to relate to people of different cultures. All of that prepared him for his future work as an urban missionary. For that to happen, we had to give him permission to go.

To say we want to let our children grow up and be on their own is one thing. Putting it into practice is something else entirely. Some parents don't really let go, and their children suffer because of it.

Helicopter Parents

Colleges such as Duke University have become aware of protective and over-involved parents. Sue Wasiolek has nearly three decades of experience working with college students and their parents.

"There is a fine line between reasonable parental concern and overbearing interference," she (Wasiolek) says, The term 'helicopter parents' is used to describe those mom and dads who constantly hover over their child, ready to swoop in whenever there is a perceived crisis. The phrase is so widely used among college administrators that one Duke official upon seeing a Duke Life Flight (medical) helicopter circling Bryan Center Plaza this fall, joked to a colleague that it surely contained Duke parents checking on their children.[2]

Schools are attempting to take a pro-active approach when it comes to ubiquitous parents. Freshmen orientation programs incorporate lessons for parents on how to separate from their students. At Colgate University in Hamilton, N.Y., administrators issue parents the university's philosophy on self-reliance when they drop off their children, according to Carline Jenkins, a spokeswoman for the university.[3]

Education professionals have even coined a new term, Black Hawk, for parents who cross the line and use unethical means, such as constructing their child's science fair project, to help their child. Even the College Board, the folks who design and oversee the Scholastic Aptitude Test (SAT), has taken notice. They report:

> In recent years, colleges have reported that helicopter parents are making their presence felt on campus. They are intervening in roommate disputes, registering their children for classes and questioning professor's grades. The consequence has been negative for students, parents and colleges.[4]

In the previous chapter we cautioned against managing the lives of our teens, rather than being consultants to them. Helicopter parents step over the line, wanting to control the lives of their teens. Such parents are not only doing their offspring a disservice by not allowing them to become independent, they risk hurting other teens. They can also destroy the relationships with those who are there to nurture their students; namely teachers, professors, and administrators.

If helicopter parents think they have their children's blessing when it comes to their behavior they are in for a surprise. In January, 2006, Experience, Inc., a leading source of career services to college students, released the results of a telephone poll involving over four hundred students and recent graduates. Twenty-five percent of those surveyed described their parents as overly involved to the point of embarrassment. Thirty-eight percent admitted their parents had become involved in their education even to the point of attending meetings with academic advisors. Thirty-one percent indicated that their parents had called professors to complain about grades.[5]

During my years as a school counselor some of my most frustrating moments came when having to deal with parents who wanted to control their student's school environment. They often stated that they only had their child's best interests at heart, but in reality they wanted to change the environment to suit what they perceived to be the needs of their child.

You Might be a Helicopter Parent if...

I truly believe none of us set out to become helicopter parents. Most of us would even be affronted at being labeled as such. The change can happen gradually. We care about our kids. As a result we can easily slip into managing and even manipulating our teen's environment.

So how do you know if you are a helicopter parent? Consider the following:

- Do you protest when your child receives a score below a ninety?

- Have you hired professional help in filling out your child's college application?
- Have you used an advisor in the college search process?
- Do you have specific expectations when it comes to your teen's college experience?
- Have you been asked to leave a meeting between you and a school official?[5]

My experience tells me that the following might also indicate that you are more involved in your teenager's life than is healthy.

You feel the need to be in constant contact with your child. When I was working as a school counselor, some of the most embarrassing moments were when a cell phone went off in a classroom and the caller was the student's parent. The school banned cell phones during the school day. They were to be in the off position and out of sight. Parents were told about the policy and it was in the school handbook, but some parents still felt the need to call their child during the school day. What I discovered was that many parents knew the policy, but still had the impulse to talk to their teen. Maybe the child had left home that morning not feeling well and the parent wanted to see how they were doing. Other times they called to find out how their student had done on a test or to get the teacher's response to a major project that had been turned in.

I must admit that even as a parent of grown children my mind shifts to thoughts of our kids. I might be sitting at my desk and suddenly I wonder what one of them might be doing at that moment. Sometimes those thoughts are filled with dread that something terrible has taken place. Such feelings are normal.

Barb and I love our kids and we check in with them regularly. We have come to recognize, however, that each of them has a life to live. We've raised them that way.

Helicopter parents have a constant need to check in. They almost always respond to the impulse to talk to their child. Whether the teen is at school, on a date, or away at camp, they feel the need to know what they are doing and how they are feeling.

You feel a need to intervene in situations on your child's behalf. It's a tough world and it is full of injustices. Our kids may be victimized sometimes. Perhaps they are the target of the school bully or treated unfairly by a teacher who seems biased against them. At such times the temptation is to want to step in and solve problems for them. Remember, we want to raise our children to be independent, self-confident adults. Ask yourself, "Is that going to happen if I am always solving their problems for them?"

What are times when you should get involved? When you have necessary information about your child the school doesn't. For example, it might be medication they are taking that is going to cause them to be drowsy or change their behavior. Other times it's a personal situation that may cause them to be distracted, such as an illness or death in the family. You might also call the school if you have a question about their policy on a particular issue. Especially call the school when your child's welfare is in danger, such as if they are being physically threatened.

There are also some times when you should not call the school. Some of those instances include when your child receives a poor or unfair grade, is cut from a school athletic team, or does not receive the part he or she wanted in the school play. When such things happen, talk through the issue at home. Shift into your role as consultant, but allow your child to handle the situation.

You feel a need to make decisions for your child. Whether the decision is big or small, teens must be allowed to make it and take ownership and responsibility for the choice. When it comes to making choices we owe them three things: 1) the information needed to make the decision (Part of that information might be our input as a consultant.); 2) the freedom and space to make the decision; 3) our unconditional love once the decision is made.

You feel negatively about yourself because of your child's failure. We cannot use our child's success to build up our own self esteem. In the same way we cannot accept responsibility, either emotional or physical, for our children's failures. If we are constantly bailing them out of difficult situations, they are learning nothing except to be dependent on us. Helicopter parents base their self-worth on their children and their accomplishments. That's just plain unhealthy.

DEVELOPING AN ACTION PLAN

We may have multiple reasons for hovering over our kids' lives, but no matter what the motive may be, the results can be harmful to everyone involved. So how do you avoid being a helicopter parent? Consider the following:

- Only get involved if you are asked and then only as a consultant. Never take ownership.

- Stay out of their personal issues. Don't get involved in personal disputes or issues involving friends, unless your child's welfare is in jeopardy.
- When it comes to finances be a coach and a role model.
- Have your own healthy lifestyle. Involve yourself in activities that are meaningful and fulfilling for you. Find your satisfaction in those.

NOTES

1. Thomas Couser, *Real Men Pray* (St. Louis: CPH, 1996), 213.
2. http://homeworktips.about.com/b/a/257778.html
3. http://www.collegeboard.com/parents/plan/getting_ready/50129.html
4. http://www.healthyplace.com/Communities/Parenting/news_2006/parenting.htm
5. http://homeworktips.about.com/b/a/277778.html

8

Mistake #7: Not Giving Our Kids Spiritual Roots

Mitch was the only child of Lynne. When he was in fourth grade, Lynne married Chuck, a man she met through her job as a dental assistant. Lynne was a devout Catholic who seldom missed Sunday mass. Mitch had been baptized in the church and always attended with her. Unlike many other children in the parish, his mother did not send him to the parish school. He went to the local public school instead. Although he really had no friends his age at church, Mitch attended confirmation classes and celebrated his First Communion when he was in third grade. Chuck, however, only attended church on holidays. With no prior father figure in his life, Mitch developed a strong relationship with his step dad.

When Mitch entered middle school his parents agreed to let him buy a guitar and take lessons. Mitch showed an almost immediate knack for the instrument. About the same time, a friend invited him to attend youth meetings at the local Baptist church. Since Lynne and Chuck agreed that Mitch should make his own decision when it came to his faith, they agreed. Before long Mitch was playing guitar for the youth choir, even traveling with them on their summer tour. Shortly after he returned home he announced to Lynne and Chuck that he had accepted Christ as his personal Savior and wanted to be baptized again. Initially Lynne was hurt, feeling that she had failed to raise him in the Catholic faith, but Chuck was quick to point out that it was Mitch's decision. "You should be happy that at least he's going to a church," he remarked.

During his sophomore year Mitch started dating Stacy, a "born-again" Christian who attended a large non-denominational church. Mitch started attending church with her and found a place in the youth praise band that led the worship for the Wednesday fellowship nights. With his good looks and pleasing personality, Mitch became a favorite among the other teens. He and Stacy were considered leaders within the group. The youth pastor, D. J., became a close friend and they often spent time on the weekends hanging out at his home with him and his wife. Stacy even babysat for the family on a regular basis.

During the summer prior to Mitch's senior year it was revealed that D. J. had been asked to resign from his position. Before a teary-eyed congregation, including most of the youth, he admitted having an affair with a woman within the church. He asked for and received forgiveness, but acknowledged that his career in the ministry was over.

Stacy and Mitch were shocked and saddened at the disclosure. At first they both felt that D. J. had betrayed them by not practicing what he preached. About two weeks later D. J. called Mitch and invited him to meet for coffee. He told Mitch that he was starting an independent youth ministry and wanted Mitch to join him as the worship leader. During the meeting he also rationalized the reason for his affair. When Mitch told Stacy she went ballistic. "How can you believe him after what he has done?" she shouted. As a result Stacy and Mitch broke up. "You can't be my friend and his, too," she proclaimed.

D. J.'s new ministry never got off the ground. He and his family ended up moving away to start over in another city. Mitch lapsed into depression. He did not want his senior year to turn out this way. Now he had lost both his girl friend and his spiritual mentor. Since neither Lynne nor Chuck had been involved in the church, neither of them could relate to Mitch or his issue. Mitch went off to college with his spiritual life in shambles and distrust toward any organized religion.

"Train up a child in the way he should go
so that when he is old he will not depart from it.

Proverbs 22:6

When God addressed his Old Testament people on the importance of spiritual roots he stated:

These commandments I give you this day are to be on your hearts. Impress them on your children. Talk about them when you sit at home and when you are walking on the road, when you lie down or when you get up. Tie them as symbols on your hand and bind them to your foreheads. Write them on the doorframes of your houses and on your gates. Deuteronomy 6:6-9

There may be some who would argue that this chapter should have come at the beginning of the book and not the end. The fact that I spent twenty-five plus years in church youth ministry, and eleven more working as a counselor at a Christian school, should be an indication of where personal spiritual growth stands as a priority in my life. In this case, I have saved the most important issue for last.

In the eyes of some I am probably an anomaly. In the past, a youth ministry position was often viewed as a stepping stone to some other form of ministry or other profession. I have watched many of my youth ministry peers move on to the seminary or graduate school. In most cases they have sought second careers as pastors, teachers, family ministers, or, in some cases, secular professions. I think part of the reason for this can be traced to the view that working with teens was not real ministry. In the past church youth ministry was viewed as entertaining youth or keeping them involved during the high school years. Sure, there were some spiritual components, but the unspoken belief was: "The youth are the future of the church, but are not a significant part of the church now." I confess that early in my ministry I fell into that trap. I could write a book on *Stupid Youth Ministry Tricks*.

In reality, youth ministry is a critical component in the spiritual development of an individual. Teens are moving from a basic Sunday school faith or rules and stories to a personal perspective of who God is and the impact that He is having on their lives.

Faith Development Theory

Jean Piaget is credited with the cognitive development theory, a premise on how children think and learn. It was the research of Erik Erikson that led to the social development theory, how people relate to each other and themselves. Lawrence Kohlberg is credited with the theory of moral development. Until the 1980's no one had published much data on spiritual development. Dr. James Fowler changed that with the release of his book, *Stages of Faith* (Harper and Row, 1981).

According to Fowler, each individual moves through clearly defined stages of spiritual development. Fowler identifies the post-puberty stage (Stage Three) as Synthetic-Conventional Faith. This stage follows Stage Two, Mythical-Literal faith. During the Mythical-Literal Stage "the person (child) begins to take on for him or herself the stories, beliefs and observances that symbolize belonging to his or her community."[1] Elementary age children who enjoy the familiar Sunday school stories are a great example of this stage. Knowing Bible stories and biblical facts should never be confused with faith and spirituality.

"Faith must synthesize values and information; must provide a basis for identity and outlook," writes Fowler. He further notes,

> It is the 'conformist stage' in the sense that it is acutely tuned to the expectations and judgments of significant others and does not have a sure enough grasp on its own identity and autonomous judgment to construct and maintain an independent personal perspective.[2]

Most teens advance from the Mythical-Literal Stage to the Synthetic-Conventional Stage. In simple terms, the Synthetic-Conventional Stage of most teens can be defined as follows. Synthetic means artificial and man-made, while conventional means traditional or the expected standard. In other words, Stage Three might be considered a veneer, only on the surface. In Jesus' parable of the sower, they would be the seeds sown on the rocky places. "But since they have not roots they last only a short time." (Mark 4:3-20)

Teenagers who have been raised in the church have received instruction and training. They have been taught basic doctrine and traditions. Many Christian denominations even celebrate the completion of this training through some right of passage, such as confirmation. *But the accumulation of knowledge about God is not faith.* Confusing a public declaration with a heart-felt testimony of faith can lead parents and church leaders into a false sense of security when it comes to youthful souls. An immature faith can be faith without roots. The nurturing process must go on. That is why church youth ministry is so vital. Teens must move from a Synthetic-Conventional faith to Stage Four, an Individual-Reflective Faith. In that stage they develop a personal perspective of God. Ultimately they must move from the traditional faith of their parents to a personal relationship with Jesus Christ.

Contemporary Youth and Their Faith

Fowler's research and theory helps us understand the various stages of faith, but his research is almost thirty years old. What about today's teens?

My experience in working with contemporary teens in a spiritual setting tends to reinforce Fowler's perspective. I have found teens to be enthusiastic about their faith. The media and the music might have changed, but the message remains the same. During the summer of 2007, I attended a national church youth gathering in Orlando, Florida, where over 25,000 teens and youth leaders gathered. This was the tenth such gathering I had attended over the span of thirty years. While the clothing and hairstyles have changed, I found this generation still committed to the faith roots of the previous generation.

Kenda Creasy Dean writes of this phenomenon in her book *Practicing Passion: Youth and the Quest for a Passionate Church*

.

> Although the brain's frontal lobes governing reason and judgment continue to develop into adulthood, by adolescence the emotional centers of the brain are well on their way to maturity, giving teenagers the propensity for leading with their hearts. In other words, the adolescent brain is wired for passion.[3]

Kenda Creasy Dean further notes the conflict that confronts teenagers pursuing a passionate faith.

> Teenagers are quick to point out the oxymoron in passionless Christianity, quick to smell danger in suppressing their emotional range, quick to question faith that fails to register on the Richter scale, and quick to abandon a church that accommodates such paltry piety. Not only does a church without passion deform theology, it inevitably extinguishes the fire behind Christian practices as well. In short, without passion, Christian faith collapses. And young people know it – which is why most of them are not spending much time in church.[4]

Search Institute's research reflects this same pursuit for passion. Involvement in a religious community and participation in youth programs were identified as positive assets. Fifty-eight percent of teens reported a connection to a religious community, fifty-seven percent noted involvement in youth programs. Experiencing these assets, along with the thirty-eight others identified by Search Institute, results in a lower involvement in at-risk behaviors.[5]

Research at the University of Illinois – Champaign further reinforces the importance of the involvement in faith-based activities.

> Religious youth groups also stand out from the classroom, part-time jobs and hanging-out with friends as context in which such (personal and interpersonal) growth occurs, the study of over 2,000 eleventh graders reported. Faith-based youth groups give teens rich opportunities for identity development, learning to relate to their emotions and developing positive relationships with peers and meaningful connections with adults… [6]

The study further reports that the teens rated the importance of participation in faith-based activities higher than sports, fine arts or other extra-curricular activities.

The pursuit of passion is what led our friend Mitch, who we met at the beginning of this chapter, to his involvement in religious youth activities. Mitch was able to unite his passion and talent for music into an activity that connected him with his peers.

This is not to say that today's youth don't have some of the same feelings of emptiness and desperate longing as other members of our society. The popularity of Rick Warren's book, *The Purpose Driven Life*, stands as a testimony to that longing.

In the opening chapter Rick Warren states, "The purpose of your life is far greater than your own personal fulfillment, your peace of mind, or even your happiness. It's far greater than your family, your career, or even your wildest dreams and ambitions."[7] Warren goes on to state that our true purpose for existence must be traced back to God's purpose for us. If you want to know why you were placed on this planet you must begin with God.

The subtitle to Warren's book is *What on Earth am I Here for?* I believe the success of his book is due in no small way to the fact that almost everyone is asking that question. Teenagers have the same deep yearning, but their lack of maturity often leads them to make poor choices about where they invest their time, energy, and passion. That is why parents need to monitor this process. More than that, though, you as a parent need to be a spiritual sojourner with your child. The strongest message that you can send your teenager is that you are a person of purpose and hope.

Walt Mueller of the Center for Parent/Youth Understanding supports this need for hope. Mueller writes in his essay, "Pass It On:"

Whether kids are consciously aware of it or not, these cries are rooted deeply in their created nature as their entire being desperately yearns to be released from the curse of sin's consequences and restored to their created place in relationship with the God who made them himself.[8]

Mueller further notes that, "In today's world it's painfully obvious that while young people are more consciously desperate in their search for fulfillment, they still aren't getting answers."[9]

In my opinion, one source for those answers is parents and other spiritual mentors. Parents need to be involved in the spiritual growth process. I am not suggesting that all parents volunteer to be youth counselors. Rather, parents need to be passing on their religious traditions and stories. They need to be open about their faith heritage and spiritual roots. They also need to admit and share their own spiritual struggles. In making themselves vulnerable in this way they are not only encouraging their children in their spiritual journey, but letting them know that it is a life-long process.

What Can We Be Doing?

In a previous chapter I spoke of the need to try to understand the needs and the culture of today's youth. That means listening to your teens and their peers. While that might result in an awareness of their needs, it does not address the issue of spiritual growth and development. So what are some practical ways to nurture spiritual growth?

Provide opportunities for growth: The church I attend recently spent 1.5 million dollars on a new student ministry addition. My initial response was, "Youth ministry wasn't like this when I was doing it." The Edge, the name the kids decided on for the new building, has all the bells and whistles. The main assembly area has a stage and features all the latest in sound and lighting equipment. There are eight breakout rooms for small groups and classes. The building even has a coffee bar where kids can gather informally, fully equipped with plug-ins for their I-pods. I can easily identify my church's commitment to youth ministry as one reason it is growing. It is a commonly accepted fact that when families are looking for a church, strong children and youth ministry programs are a high priority.

NOT GIVING OUR KIDS SPIRITUAL ROOTS

Contemporary youth ministry facilities must be built with the needs of contemporary youth in mind. They also must model the high-tech world our kids live in.

Mentors: Youth ministry traditionally has been viewed by church professionals as a stepping-stone to something else. I spent twenty-five years in church youth ministry prior to becoming a high school counselor. Even when I was forty, however, I know people still wondered what I was going to do when I grew up. Within some denominations being a youth pastor is a pre-requisite to becoming a senior pastor.

I know now how ill-equipped I was as a young youth minister. I had lots of energy and enthusiasm, but not a lot of spiritual maturity. Still, I was called to lead a youth group that numbered over one hundred. I often remarked that my first book on youth ministry should have been titled, *Father Forgive Me Because I Don't Know What I Am Doing!* I survived, and yes, most of the kids turned out fine. I still have to wonder why we typically look to young adults to serve as youth leaders.

I see three criteria when it comes to youth ministry professionals. First, they must view it as ministry in and of itself, not a stepping stone to something else. Second, they must be spiritually focused and mature themselves. Third, they must love kids.

It can't stop with the full-time staff, however. Youth ministry cannot happen within a vacuum. The hiring of a youth ministry professional is only the first step. The church must be a multi-generational community where members of all ages share their faith. It is the responsibility of all members of the church family to pass on their heritage of faith. Such communities not only provide a nurturing environment for teens and their families but allow older members to share their faith stories with the young as well. Such a church is intentional in providing opportunities for people of all generations to celebrate who they are as people of God and to learn from each other.

Model: Spiritual maturity needs to begin with us as parents. I am convinced that one reason that I eventually entered full-time church work was because of my parents. My dad was an accountant and my mother a stay-at-home mom. Church was a focal-point in our family. Sunday school and church were not an option. My dad was the Sunday school superintendent; what choice did I have? Church and faith issues were part of our family conversation. I saw both of my parents reading the scriptures and then putting it into practice. Even on his death bed my dad continued to mentor me. We shared meaningful stories, read the scripture and sang hymns together during the last week I spent with him. He faced death with a sense of hope, in the same way he faced other transitions and challenges in life.

Our faith in Jesus Christ must be the cornerstone on which our lives are built. It needs to be at the center of our family life as well. We need to pass on the heritage of faith. Ultimately, faith in Christ is the only real hope that we have.

DEVELOPING AN ACTION PLAN

I recently had dinner with a good friend and his wife. Earlier in the year they had relocated from Texas to a town in the Midwest. Their youngest child will be a junior in high school. That's a difficult time to move a child. (Our oldest son, Peter, always reminds us of that because he was in high school when we moved from Illinois to Texas.) My friend's son had attended a Lutheran High School, and they looked for a similar school in their new location. He noted that there were three options, and they allowed their son to select the school he would attend. Once that was accomplished they visited Lutheran Churches in the area and allowed him to decide where he felt most comfortable. Part of my friend's willingness to allow his son to make those choices was to ease the transition. Part of the motivation was his desire to see his son in a nurturing environment.

Provide a Nurturing Environment

Providing a nurturing environment needs to be a goal of every parent. During those critical years when our kids are experiencing adolescence, we need to be assured that they are in as nurturing an environment as possible. That might even mean putting our needs aside in favor of where they feel most comfortable. A nurturing family life is strengthened by the unity of a shared faith life. In his book *The 7 Habits of Highly Effective Families*, Stephen Covey writes, "Research also clearly shows that worshiping together is one of the major characteristics of healthy, happy families. It can create a context, unity and shared understanding…"[12]

Covey also warns against a culture that is extremely strict and sets unrealistically high expectations. He notes:

But when the environment is focused on growth based moral principles rather than on an outward perfectionism that reinforces rule-bound rigidity, people experience great health. The culture allows for honest recognition of moral imperfections and acceptance of self, even as it encourages acceptance of and living in harmony with the principles that govern all of life.[13]

Become Involved in the Church

Once the decision is made to join a church, immerse yourself in the life of that church. Get to know the staff people. Participation as a family is important. Especially involve yourself in a small group so that you develop a support network and in Bible study so that you are growing in your faith.

Get to know the youth ministry staff, both the paid staff and volunteers who work with them. Stay in touch with what is going on by reading any publicity or newsletters. Watch the adult leaders interact with youth and the way the youth react to them.

Support the youth ministry program. It takes financial support to run a modern youth ministry program. Your gifts to the Lord, in support of your church, are one way to support the youth ministry, but don't assume that the necessary resources are being allocated from the church budget. Monitor the youth budget, including the salary of the professional staff. Make sure that professional growth and support are encouraged. Finally, volunteer yourself when the appeal is put out for parental involvement.

Be a Spiritual Sojourner Yourself

Become involved in spiritual growth and Bible study on a personal level. Become part of a small group and also attend Bible classes provided by the church. Set aside time each day for personal Bible study, as well.

NOT GIVING OUR KIDS SPIRITUAL ROOTS

There is no greater model of the Christian faith than a Christian home. Be open and honest about your own spirituality, even if you struggle with it at times. Use one on one time with your teenagers to talk about spiritual issues. Let them know that you consider their spiritual development to be as important as their physical, emotional and academic development.

The bottom line is that investing in the spiritual development of your children should be even more important than investing in their college educations. A college education can certainly be important in making a difference in the earthly future. Their spiritual development, however, is an even longer term investment. It makes a difference for eternity.

NOTES

1. James Fowler, *Stages of Faith* (San Francisco: Harper & Row, 1981), 149.
2. Ibid., 170-171.
3. Kendra Creasy Dean, *Practicing Passion: Youth and their Quest for a Passionate Church* (Grand Rapids, Cambridge: Eerdmans Publishing Co., 2004), 6.
4. Ibid., 7.
5. http://www.search-institute.org/research/assets/assetfreqs.html
6. http://www.eurekaalert.org/pub_releases/2006-11/uoia-fyg110106.php
7. Rick Warren, *The Purpose Driven Life* (Grand Rapids: Zondervan Publishing, 2001),17.
8. http://cpyu.org/Page_p.aspx?id=77268
9. Ibid.

10. Ratcliff, Donald, *Adolescent Spiritual Development*

11. Stephen R. Covey, *The 7 Habits of Highly Effective Families* (New York: Franklin Covey Co., 1997), 300.

12. Ibid.

9

Seeing the Big Picture

I was a high school junior. We were a middle class family. My parents pinched pennies in order to send me to a Lutheran high school. I was an average student who ran on the track and cross country teams. I was also very immature for my age when it came to decision making. As a result, I sometimes got involved in the schemes and the at-risk behaviors of my peers.

Our family car was a 1959 nine-passenger Chevy station wagon. One of the features of the car was a rear-facing third seat that we referred to as the "poop deck." The ability to cram nine, and admittedly sometimes more, teenagers into a single vehicle made me popular on the weekend. My dad and I were the only drivers in the family, so I was allowed access to it.

My parents had rules, however. 1) They had to know where I was going. 2) They had to know who I was going to be with. 3) I had to have a definite plan that met their approval or "no car." Using the car on Friday night to attend the football game with a date was permissible. Using the car to hang-out with my buddies and cruise the local drive-ins was not.

PARENTING WITHOUT GUILT

On one particular Friday night I lied to my parents to get access to the car. I told them I had a date and was going to the basketball game at school. In actuality I was picking up eight male friends and we had no particular agenda, except to stop by the game briefly so that my story was not a complete lie. I knew I was deceiving my parents. I also knew there was going to be alcohol involved. At least I had the good judgment to not indulge myself, but I laughed plenty at the antics of my inebriated friends. Along the way we got ourselves in some trouble and the police got involved. Fortunately, the damage was minor. I did most of the talking, so the police never caught on to the fact that most of my friends were drunk. No one was arrested or even ticketed, but I knew my parents were going to find out.

As a result, I stood with two friends in our living room in front of dad at midnight and confessed what I had done. My friends rationalized that if they were with me my dad wouldn't yell too loudly. My dad listened to the story and then responded with, "We can discuss this in the morning. Right now you need to get your friends home."

"Your dad was so cool," both of my friends gushed in reference to his calm demeanor.

I, however, knew what that Saturday morning conversation was going to be like. My dad was forgiving, but there would be consequences. My dad's intent was that I learn from my mistakes. A few years back I spent time with him on his death bed. It was there he finally admitted that I did try his patience, reminding me that I was a "late bloomer."

SEEING THE BIG PICTURE

My restrictions from using the car were open-ended. My dad wanted me to think long and hard about what had happened. About six weeks later I wanted to borrow the car to take a girl to a dance. I asked for the car and gained permission, but it came with some new restrictions. In addition to the previous rules -- where, who and what -- I now was instructed to call home periodically and report in. This was especially the case if plans changed or I was going to be even five minutes late. These were the days long before cell phones, so I always kept change in my pocket for the pay phone. It was a rare night when I didn't check in with my folks at least once or twice. My dad never mentioned the drinking episode again.

When it came to parenting my dad was definitely a "big picture" guy. I suspect he didn't know much psychology or developmental theory. For sure, he knew nothing about the development of the pre-frontal cortex and its role in decision making. He just expected me to grow up and somewhere along the line make better choices. He was almost always the consultant. I knew exactly what he was thinking because he had told me. Almost everyone else, including my friends, was shocked when I announced my intent to go to Concordia Teachers College in preparation for full-time ministry. My dad just smiled. Being a big picture person, he knew that I was a basically good kid who had made poor choices. I had been nurtured in the faith and Christian principles. Somewhere along the line I would begin to put things together and make some good choices.

As a school counselor I saw similar things happen countless times. A student who had made poor choices early in his or her high school career went on to be successful. Perhaps it was the young man who abused alcohol as a sophomore who went on to graduate with a MBA from a prestigious university in the northeast. Maybe it was the girl who skipped the prom her junior year because she was pregnant, who now is a nurse with a family of her own.

There will always be kids who are easy to love. They are the athletes who are also members of the National Honor Society or the student leaders who go on to attend prominent universities. I, however, found the greatest satisfaction in helping the kids who struggled just to get to the point where they would walk across the stage to receive their diplomas. Some of them would go off to college. Others would enroll in a community college close to home. Some of them enlisted in the armed forces. Others would work full-time. Most of them had a plan. With that plan in place they were moving forward with a sense of purpose and with enthusiasm.

As parents we need to see the big picture. So often we focus on the mistakes of the moment instead of the potential that is in the future. How can we help our teens to learn from their present circumstance, using that as a building block instead of an obstacle?

Help them learn from their mistakes. When our teens make mistakes or let us down, the initial reaction is to focus on the act. It could be that it put them in danger, or perhaps they embarrassed us. As a result we want to make sure it doesn't happen again. Punishment is seen as a deterrent. We might also want to draw attention to how their actions have impacted others, including ourselves.

While there need to be consequences, we cannot allow the teachable moment to slip by. A good way to make sure that happens is to gather all the facts and then walk them through the event. Listen to their thought process and how the decision was made. Help them to consider other options they might have had.

I have discovered that teens sometimes considered making better choices, but for one reason or another went in a different direction. In such cases they were probably closer to doing the right thing than what I originally gave them credit for. By walking them through the process they might even gain an understanding as to why appropriate consequences are needed. Perhaps we might discover that they are harder on themselves than we intended to be.

Learn to forgive. There can be no greater model of the Christian faith than a Christian family. God forgives us for Jesus' sake and expects us to do the same. The love for our kids must be unconditional, in the same way God's love for us knows no bounds. Forgiveness does not mean there aren't consequences. Love, however, must always be the motive.

Focus on the future and not the past. Once a mistake is made, let it go and move on. Nothing is accomplished by constantly saying, "And remember the time you..." In the same way we don't want to be constantly reminded of stupid things we have done, our kids don't want to be reminded, either.

Help them set goals. My experience is that people who are focused on long-term goals tend to make better choices. They want to avoid doing things that could hinder their progress toward where they want to go. The sooner we can help our kids cast a vision for their future, the sooner they will begin to make decisions that will move them toward that goal. While serious college and career planning usually begins during the junior year in high school, it is never too early to help teens discover the gifts and interests that they have. Once those gifts have been identified we can help them discover career options using those gifts. Use your circle of friends to help you identify adults who might be in those professions who can mentor your teens in those fields.

Allow them to pursue their dreams. It's interesting that both of our boys had dreams of being sports broadcasters. Peter graduated from Texas Christian University with a degree in Radio-TV-Film. He did baseball play-by-play in college and then got a job doing football play-by-play for an independent production company. Mark had his own local radio show when he was still in high school and continued that at Valparaiso University. His claim to fame in college was as the arena voice for the women's volleyball and basketball teams. Barb and I gave all three of our children the opportunity to pursue their dreams. The fact that Peter and Mark both ended up in some form of ministry was their decision, although the Holy Spirit was working through them, too. Barb and I didn't want them to say, "I always wanted to do that, but you wouldn't let me." The dreams of youth might be totally unrealistic, but no one, especially a parent, should ever say that they are impossible. Everyone deserves the opportunity to reach for the stars.

And so...

I began this book with the thought that being the parent of a teenager can be scary and frustrating. It can also be exciting and gratifying. As the parents of three adult children, Barb and I get great satisfaction in watching our kids use their gifts in service to others and living out God's plan. My prayer is that each of you can have a similar experience. There is no greater joy than watching your adult children grow to be responsible, capable adults of faith and strong character. Parenting does take a conscious effort, though. I hope what I have offered can help you toward the goal of raising independent and successful young adults. As you travel the road, remember that God goes with you. He will give you the wisdom and insight needed to face the challenges. He will also forgive your mistakes. God bless your great adventure!

Parenting without Guilt Study Guide

INTRODUCTION

GETTING STARTED

1. What do you find to be the greatest joy when it comes to raising children? What is the biggest challenge?
2. How are things different now than when you were the age of your kids?

SOME REALITIES ABOUT TODAY'S KIDS

1. Kids run the extremes when it comes to _____. They also lack to _____ and _____ to deal with them.
2. Today's kids experience puberty _____ an previous generations.
3. Teenagers are wired differently. Their brains lack the ability to make _____ _____.

PARENTING WITHOUT GUILT

Read Ephesians 6:1-4

1. What makes being obedient the right thing to do when it comes to children and their parents? The command begins with the word, "honor." Is honor something that should be randomly given? How does a person earn honor?
2. How do fathers and mothers exasperate their children? Can you think of a time when you frustrated your child?
3. Verse 4 contains the adverb "instead," implying that something must take the place of another. What is being replaced and what is put in its place?

What role does Christian training play in this?

Bad Parenting

Examine the following scripture references. How are they examples of bad parenting? What mistakes did the parents make? What could have been done differently? What can you learn from the story?

Genesis 25:19-34
Genesis 27:1-17
I Samuel 8:1-5
I Kings 1:5-6

"The rod of correction impart wisdom,
but a child left to itself disgraces his mother."

Proverbs 29:15

Mistake #1: Confusing Discipline with Punishment

GETTING STARTED

1. Describe your family growing up. What style of parenting did your parents use? Did they have any unique ways of punishing you and your siblings?
2. What style of parenting do you and your spouse if married, use? How did you decide what forms of punishment to use?
3. How does your parenting style compare with that of your parents?

DEFINING DISCIPLINE

1. What is the intended goal of punishment?
2. How are consequences different from punishment?
3. What is the intended goal of discipline?

READ HEBREWS 12:1-13

1. How does God use discipline to shape His disciples? Can you think of a specific time in your life when you felt God was disciplining you?
2. According to vs. 7 what does the author see as a requirement in parenting?
3. According to vs. 9 what happens as a result of a parent disciplining a child?
4. On our walk of discipleship, where should our focus be? (vs. 1-3)

PARENTING WITHOUT GUILT

READ JOHN 8:1-11

1. The sin here is adultery. The woman has been caught in the act. What was the punishment supposed to be?
2. How did the religious leaders view the situation? How did Jesus view it?
3. The religious leaders recognized the sin of the woman, does Jesus as well?
4. How do we know that?
5. Jesus makes it clear that the woman is not condemned because of her offense. That does not mean there were not consequences. What might some of those consequences be?
6. What can we, as parents, learn from this situation that we can apply to our own parenting?

READ EXODUS 20:1-21

1. How does the world view these commandments today? Should that affect our perspective on them?
2. As New Testament Christians, The Ten Commandments are to be our guide in leading lives of discipleship, as well as exposing our sin. In setting boundaries for your child which ones would you make the highest priority?
3. Which commandments will you focus on personally?

"Whoever loves discipline loves knowledge,
but he who hates correction is stupid."

Proverbs 12:1

Mistake #2: A Failure to Communicate

GETTING STARTED

1. How was the communication between you and your parents growing up? What opportunity did you have for family communication? (Examples might be time in the care traveling or the dinner hour)?
2. What affect does society have on the communication in your home? What activities pull family members away?

DEFINING COMMUNICATION

1. Communication is the giving or receiving of information or news by speaking, writing, gesture or other means. (Scott, Foresman Advanced Dictionary)
2. What form of communication do you tend to rely on the most? Why? Is that method always the most effective way to communicate with your teen?
3. When it comes to receiving information are you better at spoken, written or visual communication?

READ JAMES 1:19-27

1. James makes communication a high priority. Why do you thing he links listening and anger? How could moral filth and prevalent evil negatively impact communication?
2. Verse 21 talks about "the word planted in you." What is that word and what affect should it have?
3. What indication do you detect that lead you to believe James thinks God holds Christians to a higher standard when it comes to communication?

4. How important is self control when it comes to communication? In Speaking?

5. In listening? In writing?

READ PROVERBS 18:2, 13

1. The author of Proverbs views communication as two-way. What are they saying about the role of listening?

2. How can they associate not listening with being "a fool" or participating in folly?

3. On a 10 point scale, how would you rate yourself as a listener? How can you become a better listener, especially as you relate to your teens?

"The heart of the discerning acquires knowledge;
the ears of the wise seek it out."

Proverbs 18:15

Mistake #3: Failure to Develop a Support System

GETTING STARTED:

1. Other than your parents, who were the significant adults in your life when you were growing up?
2. Who were your mentors? What made them good mentors for you?
3. Share a memory of a time when your mentor was particularly helpful?

DEFINING A MENTOR

According to Greek Legend, Mentor was a faithful friend of Ulysses. A mentor is a wise and trusted advisor. (Scott, Foresman Advanced Dictionary)

1. What does it take to be a good mentor?
2. What characteristics do mentors need to have?

READ EPHESIANS 4:11-16

1. Paul identifies four specific spiritual gifts. How might people with those gifts serve as mentors? Does possessing the gifts guarantee that a person can be a mentor? What might prevent that?
2. What is the purpose of all gifts according to Paul? (vs. 12-13)
3. What long-term benefits does the person being mentored receive? (vs. 14-16)

PARENTING WITHOUT GUILT

FOR MORE ON SPIRITUAL GIFTS READ ROMANS 12:1-8

What additional spiritual gifts does Paul identify here?

What does Paul see as the objective for all disciples of Christ? (vs. 1-2)

What challenges do followers of Christ face in their attempts to be "living sacrifices?"

How might meeting those challenges make you a better mentor or role model? How might they detract from that role?

Mentors in Your Teens World

1. Outside of immediate family, who are the significant adults in your teen's world? Do you view their influence as being positive or negative?
2. If the adults in your teen's world are playing a positive role, what can you do to encourage that relationship?
3. If your teen is lacking adult mentors what can you do to change that?

"The discerning heart seeks knowledge,
but the mouth of a fool feeds on folly."

Proverbs 15:14

Mistake #4: Living Your Dreams Vicariously through Our Kids

GETTING STARTED

1. What kind of extra-curricular activities were you involved in during your teenage years? What kind of role did you play in that activity? (Example: member of basketball team or treasurer of the drama club) What level of success did you have?

2. What kind of activities is your teenager involved in? How does their involvement compare to yours at the same age?

3. What motivated you to be involved in extra-curricular activities? If you asked your teen what motivates them, how do you think they would respond? What really motivates today's teens to be involved in extra-curricular activities?

READ PHILIPPIANS 2:1-4

1. According to Paul, what should motivate followers of Christ? What should not motivate them?

2. Whose interest should be first in our lives? How can we become encouragers?

READ PHILIPPIANS 2:5-11

1. What model does Paul present for humility?

2. What was Jesus' motivation?

3. What can we learn from that?

REFLECTING ON OUR DREAMS FOR OUR KIDS

1. Think back on your child's infancy. What dreams did you

have for your child in their early years? How did you picture them as a teenager and as an adult? How does your early image of your child as a teen compare to them today?

2. What do you perceive as your child's strongest attributes? What are their weaknesses? What are you doing to help them build on their strengths and overcome their weaknesses?

Take Time

1. Have an honest discussion with your teenager about their future. What skills and interests do they see themselves as having? What career interests do they have? How do those dreams match-up with their gifts?

2. What can you be doing now help they realize their dreams?

> "A man is praised according to his wisdom,
> but men with warped minds are despised."

Proverbs 12:8

Mistake #5: Being a Manager Rather than a Consultant

GETTING STARTED

1. Who are the people you turn to for advice at this time in your life?
2. Who were the people you looked to for advice during your teen years?
3. In your mind, what does it take to be a good consultant?

READ 2 TIMOTHY 2:22-26

1. Paul writes about, "fleeing the evil desires of youth..." What expectations does Paul have for adults?
2. Paul instructs Timothy to avoid "stupid arguments and quarrels." How can we become contentious in our roles as consultants?
3. What hope does Paul offer for offer to consultants who find their advice ignored? How might this be comforting to the parents of teens?

READ 1 KINGS 12:1-16

1. In this story Rehoboam consults two groups of advisors. Which group does he listen to? Why does he heed their advice rather than the other opinion? What was the result?
2. Why do children and teens at times spurn what we perceive as good advice for bad? What can we do when this takes place?
3. What ultimately should be the constants in our relationship with our child?

Moving Forward

1. What current issue in your child's world do you feel you best equipped to be a consultant? How open are they to that advice? What can you do to build a bridge so that they might be open and accepting to your counsel?

2. Who are other significant adults in your teen's life who might share the same recommendation? What can you do to cultivate your child's relationship with that person?

"Starting a quarrel is like breaching a dam;
so drop the matter before a dispute breaks out."

Proverbs 17:14

Mistake #6: Not Letting Go

GETTING STARTED

1. Reflect back on what it was like when you left home for the first time (Examples: Left for college, military, first job away from home, etc.). How did you feel about leaving? How did your parents react? How did they express their feelings?
2. What have you done to mentally prepare yourself for your child's departure from your home?

READ 1 SAMUEL 1:21-28

1. Background: (1 Samuel 1:1-20) Elkanah and Hannah had waited a long time for the birth of their first son. God finally answered their prayers and Hannah gave birth to Samuel.
2. What motivated Hannah to act as she did?
3. Hannah waited until after Samuel had been weaned. How would that have made giving him over to the Lord more difficult?
4. Hannah was a very spiritually focused and dedicated woman. What role does our spiritually play in our parenting, especially when it comes to letting our children go?

READ LUKE 2:41-50

1. The age twelve must have marked the transition from being a child to adulthood for Jesus, since he was allowed to visit Jerusalem with his parents for the first time. Today a Jewish boy's Bar Mitzvah today marks the same right of passage. Formal religious training is complete and boys are considered to be an adult. In Jesus day it marked the transition into

vocational training, when a father would mentor his son in his profession.

2. What indications are there that Jesus was ready to function on his own?

3. What emotions did Mary and Joseph experience at the realization that Jesus might be in Jerusalem on his own? How might they be similar to the feelings parents have when they let their children go today?

4. How did Jesus respond to his parent's concern? How do would you expect your child to respond?

Letting Go

1. How do we know when it is time to let our teens go today?

2. What can we be doing right now to prepare them and ourselves for that day?

"Sons are a heritage from the Lord, children a reward from Him.
Like arrows in the hand of a warrior are the sons of ones youth.
Blessed is the man whose quiver is full of them.
They will not be put to shame when they contend with their enemies in the gate."

Psalm 127:3-5

Mistake #7: Not Giving Our Kids Spiritual Roots

GETTING STARTED

1. Reflect on your own spiritual development. Who were the people who mentored you in your faith?
2. When did you first begin to establish a personal relationship with Christ? What event or events led to that?

READ DEUTERONOMY 6:1-25

1. Deuteronomy literary means the "Second Law." A full generation had passed since the Exodus from Egypt and the subsequent dramatic crossing of the Red Sea. The author, usually considered to be Moses, wanted to remind the Children of Israel of God's actions and His expected response from his people. A review of the Ten Commandments had preceded this chapter.
2. (vs. 1-3) What did God command Moses to do? What was God intended purpose? How would the people benefit from obedience to God's commands?
3. (vs. 4-9) The theme in verse 4 is repeated throughout the New Testament (see Luke 10:27 & Matthew 22:37). How does this relate to parents and those who work with children and youth? How does it happen?
4. (vs. 10-12) What dangers did Moses foresee once the people had reached the Promised Land? How do parents face similar dangers in today's world?
5. (vs. 20-25) What responsibility is placed on parents? How does that happen today?
6. God had certain expectations for the Children of Israel once they reached the Promised Land (vs. 18-19). Moses

goes into greater detail in Chapter 7. What was expected? How should contemporary Christian parents respond to God's command and warnings?

Providing Roots:

1. What kind of nurturing environment have you created for your children as they grow in their faith?
2. What stories do you have about your own spiritual development that you can share with your children? How can you create an environment where that can be shared?
3. As you look to the future, beyond high school, how can you insure that the spiritual development continues?

"Train up a child in the way he should go,
and when he is old he will not depart from it."

Proverbs 22:6

PARENTING WITHOUT GUILT STUDY GUIDE

Seeing the Big Picture - Part 1

GETTING STARTED

1. What were your dreams during your senior year in high school? Who were the people who shared your dream and helped you work toward it? How realistic was your dream?

2. Compare your life now with the dream that you had. What parts of the dream has been fulfilled? What parts of the dream are unfulfilled?

3. What dreams do your children have? What role have you played in establishing those dreams?

4. Why is it important that each person have the opportunity to pursue any realistic plan for their future?

READ GENESIS 15:1-20

1. What was the source of Abram's (Abraham's) vision? What promise came with the vision?

2. Abram had some concerns over how realistic the vision was. What were they? What was God's response to the concerns?

3. How was the vision of the future revealed to Abram? According to verse 6, how did Abram respond to the vision? What additional benefit did he receive? (see Hebrews 11:8-12)

4. What role should God play in setting our vision and the vision of our children? How can we as parents facilitate that?

5. Scan Numbers 13 and 14. Read Numbers 13:26-33, 14:5-9 and 14:24.

6. Joshua and Caleb had a very different perspective than their peers. What was the source of their vision? How realistic was it from their peer's point of view? Why do you think they got it but their peers didn't?

7. How can we cultivate an attitude like Joshua's and Caleb's among our children?

8. What blessings did Joshua and Caleb receive? What blessing might our children receive? What blessings might we receive as parents?

"Be happy, young man, while you are young,
and let your heart give you joy in the days of your youth.
Follow the ways of your heart and whatever your eyes see.
but know that in all things God will bring you to judgment."

Ecclesiastes 11:9

Seeing the Big Picture - Part 2

GETTING STARTED

1. When have you experienced forgiveness on a personal level in your life? How did it feel to be forgiven by someone?

2. Do you feel differently when you are the person who is being forgiven, as opposed to those times when you are the victim and have to forgive someone else?

LUKE 23:32-34

1. Considering what had happened prior to this, how would we have expected a normal person to react? Why do we expect a normal person to react with anger and vindictiveness?

2. What was the source of Jesus compassion toward the crowd that mostly consisted to His accusers?

3. We pray in the Lord's Prayer, "Forgive us our sins and as we forgive those who sin against us." This petition is rooted in Jesus' words from the cross. Saying these words are one thing, putting them into action is difficult. What are the obstacles that keep us from being forgiving? Within the context of a family, what are the implications if we do not practice forgiveness?

4. Does being forgiven totally let a person off the hook in terms of their responsibility to others? To God?

LUKE 15:11-31

1. What words would you use to describe the father in this story?

2. What parable preceded this one? What message do you

think Jesus was trying to teach us through these stories?

3. What were the son's expectations as he returned home? How was the outcome not what he expected?

4. The implication in terms of our relationship with your own children is obvious. Does this mean things will always turn out good? Why won't some people understand?

A Spirit of Forgiveness needs to be at the heart of all relationships, especially within a Christian family.

CPSIA information can be obtained
at www.ICGtesting.com
Printed in the USA
LVHW051541030419
612806LV00012BA/497/P